Quality Management of Cultural Heritage: problems and best practices

Proceedings of the XVII UISPP World Congress (1–7 September 2014, Burgos, Spain)

Volume 8 / Session A13

Edited by

Maurizio Quagliuolo and Davide Delfino

Archaeopress Archaeology

Archaeopress Publishing Ltd
Gordon House
276 Banbury Road
Oxford OX2 7ED

www.archaeopress.com

ISBN 978 1 78491 295 6
ISBN 978 1 78491 296 3 (e-Pdf)

© Archaeopress, UISPP and authors 2016

VOLUME EDITORS: Maurizio Quagliuolo and Davide Delfino

SERIES EDITOR: The board of UISPP

SERIES PROPERTY: UISPP – International Union of Prehistoric and Protohistoric Sciences

The editing of this volume was funded by the Instituto Terra e Memória, Centro de Geociências UID/Multi/00073/2013, with the support of the Fundação para a Ciência e Tecnologia FCT/MEC)

KEY-WORDS IN THIS VOLUME: Quality Management; Heritage; Landscape Management; Archeological sites; Valorization

UISPP PROCEEDINGS SERIES is a printed on demand and an open access publication, edited by UISPP through Archaeopress

BOARD OF UISPP: Jean Bourgeois (President), Luiz Oosterbeek (Secretary-General), François Djindjian (Treasurer), Ya-Mei Hou (Vice President), Marta Arzarello (Deputy Secretary-General). The Executive Committee of UISPP also includes the Presidents of all the international scientific commissions (www.uispp.org)

BOARD OF THE XVII WORLD CONGRESS OF UISPP: Eudald Carbonell (Secretary-General), Robert Sala I Ramos, Jose Maria Rodriguez Ponga (Deputy Secretary-Generals)

All rights reserved. No part of this book may be reproduced, or transmitted, in any form or by any means, electronic, mechanical, photocopying or otherwise, without the prior written permission of the copyright owners.

This book is available direct from Archaeopress or from our website www.archaeopress.com

Content

List of Figures and Tables ii

Foreword to the XVII UISPP Congress Proceedings Series Edition v
Luiz OOSTERBEEK

Introduction iv
Maurizio QUAGLIUOLO and Davide DELFINO

Quality Management at World Heritage sites: challenges 1
Maurizio QUAGLIUOLO

**Landscape destruction and heritage mismanagement in Murujuga
(Western Australia)** 3
José Antonio GONZALEZ ZARANDONA

**Media strategies observed in the Portuguese press to save Vila Nova de Foz Côa engravings.
A case study on socialization of the archaeological heritage** 13
Cinta S. BELLMUNT

**Archaeological research and applied arts for Public Archaeology in a Final Bronze Age
hilltop walled station of Castelo Velho da Zimbreira (Mação-Portugal)** 21
Davide DELFINO, Dragos GHEORGHIU and Livia STEFAN

**Virtual palimpsests: augmented reality and the use of mobile devices to visualise
the archaeological record** 35
Dragoş GHEORGHIU and Livia ŞTEFAN

**Conservation, Preservation and Site Management at the Neanderthal Sites at
Veldwezelt-*Hezerwater*, Belgium** 49
Patrick M. M. A. BRINGMANS

**The scientific value of replicas through the analytic experience of
Magdalenian portable art** 59
Roberto ÁVILA

List of Figures and Tables

J. A. Gonzalez Zarandona: **Landscape destruction and heritage mismanagement in Murujuga (Western Australia)**

Figure 1. Until the natural resources are exhausted, the mining industry will not leave Murujuga 4

C. S. Bellmunt: **Media strategies observed in the Portuguese press to save Vila Nova de Foz Côa engravings. A case study on socialization of the archaeological heritage**

Figure 1. Geographical location 14
Figure 2. Most of the figures craved in Foz Côa represent animals 14
Figure 3. Big camp in Foz Côa 17
Figure 4. Mário Soares in Foz Côa whit students 18

D. Delfino, D. Gheorghiu and L. Stefan: **Archaeological research and applied arts for Public Archaeology in a Final Bronze Age hilltop walled station of Castelo Velho da Zimbreira (Mação-Portugal)**

Figure 1. System of territory settlement in the Final Bronze Age in the Council of Mação 22
Figure 2. Hill top walled station of Castelo Velho da Zimbreira 23
Figure 3. Stratigraphic section of the interior of wall 2 24
Figure 4. Working in progress during the performance of Land Art in Castelo Velho da Zimbreira 26
Figure 5. Placing the white tissue of the Land Art up the wall of Castelo Velho da Zimbreira 27
Figure 6. The fireplaces at Castelo Velho da Zimbreira, Castelo Velho do Caratão, Castro do Santo 27
Figure 7. Gathering at Castelo Velho da Zimbreira around the fireplace 28
Figure 8. Students at work during the 2012 campaign 29
Figure 9. The QR Code for starting the mobile AR application and display of 3D reconstructions 30
Figure 10. Images of the recreated walled station can also be seen on a mobile phone by scanning 30
Table 1. Categories and numbers of visitors at the Castelo Velho da Zimbreira 31

D. Gheorghiu and L. Ştefan: **Virtual palimpsests: augmented reality and the use of mobile devices to visualise the archaeological record**

Figure 1. The prehistoric road. Vădastra village, Romania 39
Figure 2. The Roman road. Vădastra village, Romania 40
Figure 3. The virtual palimpsest using Google Maps custom layers 41
Figure 4. Capture from the "ar-palimpsest" AR mobile application 41
Figure 5. An augmented Google Maps POI (the prehistoric layer) 42
Figure 6. An augmented Google Maps POI (the Roman layer) 43
Figure 7. A LOI in the ar-palimpsest application 44
Figure 8. Demo of the mobile virtual palimpsest at the XVIIth World UISPP Congress Burgos 45
Figure 9. Interactive Map at the XVII World UISPP 2014 Congress Burgos September 2014 45

P. M. M. A. Bringmans: **Conservation, Preservation and Site Management at the Neanderthal Sites at Veldwezelt-Hezerwater, Belgium**

Figure 1. Location of the Neanderthal sites at Veldwezelt-*Hezerwater* (Belgium) 50
Figure 2. Visitors participating in guided walking tours at the Veldwezelt-*Hezerwater* sites 53
Figure 3. The main geological profile at Veldwezelt-*Hezerwater* 54
Figure 4. A Neanderthal and an Anatomically Modern Human walking side by side *56*

R. Ávila: **The scientific value of replicas through the analytic experience of Magdalenian portable art**

Table 1. Number of replicated objects sorted by their condition. 62
Figure 1. Artefact usually denominated "Contour Decoupé" made of hyoid bones 63
Figure 2. Artefact usually denominated "Bâton Percé", made on antler 65
Figure 3. Artefact with no apparent function made on a mandible of cervid 66
Figure 4. Flowchart of an exhaustive documentation related to portable art replicas 68

Foreword to the XVII UISPP Congress Proceedings Series Edition

Luiz OOSTERBEEK
Secretary-General

UISPP has a long history, starting with the old International Association of Anthropology and Archaeology, back in 1865, until the foundation of UISPP itself in Bern, in 1931, and its growing relevance after WWII, from the 1950's. We also became members of the International Council of Philosophy and Human Sciences, associate of UNESCO, in 1955.

In its XIVth world congress in 2001, in Liège, UISPP started a reorganization process that was deepened in the congresses of Lisbon (2006) and Florianópolis (2011), leading to its current structure, solidly anchored in more than twenty-five international scientific commissions, each coordinating a major cluster of research within six major chapters: Historiography, methods and theories; Culture, economy and environments; Archaeology of specific environments; Art and culture; Technology and economy; Archaeology and societies.

The XVIIth world congress of 2014, in Burgos, with the strong support of Fundación Atapuerca and other institutions, involved over 1700 papers from almost 60 countries of all continents. The proceedings, edited in this series but also as special issues of specialized scientific journals, will remain as the most important outcome of the congress.

Research faces growing threats all over the planet, due to lack of funding, repressive behavior and other constraints. UISPP moves ahead in this context with a strictly scientific programme, focused on the origins and evolution of humans, without conceding any room to short term agendas that are not root in the interest of knowledge.

In the long run, which is the terrain of knowledge and science, not much will remain from the contextual political constraints, as severe or dramatic as they may be, but the new advances into understanding the human past and its cultural diversity will last, this being a relevant contribution for contemporary and future societies.

This is what UISPP is for, and this is also why we are currently engaged in contributing for the relaunching of Human Sciences in their relations with social and natural sciences, namely collaborating with the International Year of Global Understanding, in 2016, and with the World Conference of the Humanities, in 2017.

The next two congresses of UISPP, in Melbourn (2017) and in Geneva (2020), will confirm this route.

Introduction

Maurizio Quagliuolo and Davide Delfino

From Lascaux to Shanidar caves, from Malta temples to Stonenge (and the 'new' one...), from Serra da Capivara to Foz Coa park, from Australia to North Africa's Rock Art, from Pechino to Isernia excavations, from the Musée de l'Homme in Paris to the Museum of Civilization in Quebéc, from Çatal Hüyük to the Varna village, from the Rift Valley to the Grand Canyon, most problems have to be fronted in a **common perspective**. But which perspective? Is it possible to have a common point of view on different values, different sites, different methodologies? The Scientific Commission for the Quality Management of Prehistoric and Protohistoric Sites, Monuments and Museums© set up at UISPP by initiative of the author (UISPP-PPCHM) is aimed to examine these issues and propose solutions acceptable to all those who want to contribute to common understanding of our past history.

The only certainty in fact is our Past. It is undoubted that it happened, it is undoubted that its consequences are in place today, it is undoubted that it is affecting persons, social groups or larger structures in some ways also when it is disregarded.

The help of specialists from different Countries and the exchange of opinions with other colleagues from other fields and/or organizations is then needed in order to:
- discuss the reasons and possibilities for preservation and use of Sites, Monuments and Museums;
- let the management of Rock Art Sites and Parks, Prehistoric excavations, Museums and Interpretations Centres and related structures open to the public to be made according to criteria agreed at an International level, both in normal and critical conditions;
- enhance standards in preserving, communicating and using Sites, Monuments and Museums;
- involve the public and diffuse awareness;
- analyse tourism benefits and risks at these destinations;
- introduce new opportunities for jobs and training;
- develop networks on these topics in connection with other specialized Organizations.

This session was aimed to know: what is your experience? Which problems would you like to address? Which solutions?

Maurizio Quagliuolo with the paper *Quality Management at World Heritage sites: challenges*, presents a global perspective about Quality and Management of Heritage and talks about the role of the Culture in a social perspective. Showing what are the priorities in improving the awareness and use of Cultural Heritage, it suggests a positive profiting of that in meliorating cultural and political network between peoples.

José António Gonzalez Zarandona with the paper *Landscape destruction and heritage mismanagement in Murujuga (Western Australia)* shows the case study of the Murujuga petroglyphs area (West Australia), one of the largest places in the world with concentration of rock art, partially destroyed by iron mining works. The surviving part is presently not interested by a rescue and valorisation project; author highlights the social importance of petroglyphs to the indigenous community and its intangible value for the world heritage enrichment and preservation.

Cinta Bellmut with the paper *Media strategies observed in the Portuguese press to save Vila Nova de Foz Côa engravings. A case study on socialization of the archaeological heritage*, presents a consideration about the social factor and the role of social communication in the rescue and valorisation of Rock Art in Côa Valley (Portugal); the action of the archaeologists in disclosing the finds to the people and the high interest arisen in the newspapers that contributed to the global awareness at rescuing rock art in Côa Valley are particularly highlighted.

Davide DELFINO, Dragos GHEORGHIU and Livia STEFAN with the paper *Archaeological research and applied arts for Public Archaeology in a Final Bronze Age hilltop walled station of Castelo Velho da Zimbreira (Mação-Portugal)* present periodic activities for the valorisation of a protohistoric monument that has not such a monumentality, but is important to the survival of the spirit of a peripheral small territory in inland Portugal. Public Archaeology has been carried out by multiple activities, involving several people of different types and using various factors of attraction based on scientific data coming from the excavations, putting the monument in special relation with the surrounding landscape.

Dragos GHEORGHIU and Livia STEFAN with the paper *Virtual palimpsests: augmented reality and the use of mobile devices to visualise the archaeological record*, present a very useful tool for archaeologists to read a multilayer context at archaeological sites using augmented reality, Google Maps and mobile devices. The case study of Vadastra (Romania) shows this virtual palimpsest applied to the multi-layer archaeological reality of Calcolithic and Iron Age structures and goods, as well as its potential successful application in a wider range of contexts in the future.

Patrick BRINGMANS with the paper *Conservation, Preservation and Site Management at the Neanderthal Sites at Veldwezelt-Hezerwater, Belgium* shows a very successful connection among field investigation, public archaeology and valorisation of a prehistoric settlement intervention project, in a special research context of ancient Neanderthal's occupation of the territory, related behavior and strategy for raw materials management; the success of Public Archaeology along some years, on the initiative by the researchers' team earned the interest of the Flemish Government, that decided to fund a project to develop it permanently.

Roberto ÁVILA with the paper *The scientific value of replicas through the analytic experience of Magdalenian portable art*, highlights the potentiality of mobile Upper Paleolithic art replicas for education, valorisation, preservation and study of the context. The author presents a replica of mobile Magdalenian art from Dordogne (France) and calls attention to the importance of the replica in relation to the fragility of the original, for using in teaching and research activities.

Quality Management at World Heritage sites: challenges

Maurizio QUAGLIUOLO
President of the UISPP-PPCHM committee,
Secretary-General of HERITY International

Well. Let's speak about Quality. Let's speak about Management. Let's speak about Culture. At present, this article could stop here.

Why?

Because nowadays, the common perspective which appears to have been shared for a long time up today according to the "Universal Value" on which the 1972 UNESCO Convention is based, seems to be no more effective.

In a more realistic way, we should ask ourselves if it is possible today to have a common point of view on different values, different sites, different approaches. It's time to examine issues related to the perception of the importance (or not) of a cultural relict before dealing with jobs related to archaeology and research, norms and laws, best practices and recognition of professionalism, history and restoration, conservation and communication, awareness and teaching, services and management, which proposals of improvement are acceptable **only** to those who share a common vision about the main subject of our efforts: the common understanding of our past history as a driver for future development.

If there is no agreement on this understanding, there is no Cultural Heritage to study, preserve, communicate and enjoy. *Global understanding* is a chimera without dialogue. Dialogue is not agreement, simply a good disposition to discuss. It seems that today this good disposition is not completely diffused.

The only certainty in fact is our Past. It is undoubted that it happened, it is undoubted that its consequences are in place today, it is undoubted that it is affecting persons, social groups or larger structures in some ways also where it is disregarded.

But when we speak about knowledge, conservation, transmission, economic development in connection with the Cultural Heritage as a **common** goal with the emphasis that is given today by UNESCO, ICCROM, specialized agencies at UN, EU (-which EU? We could say-) or non-governmental international organizations such as ICOMOS, ICOM, Europa Nostra or Private Funds devoted to cultural heritage protection and diffusion, we should at first ask ourselves if anyone of the actors (or *stakeholders*) agrees on:
Which value?
Why preserve?
How to communicate the message(s) -if any is recognized-?
Should we have services at the site (if visited!)?

I already wrote in other essays about the Mostar bridge, about the Buddha statues in Afghanistan etc. and their relation with the historical conquerors dealing with different civilizations, destroying symbols and killing people in ancient times. As archaeologists and Historians we should know these facts very well. This is why I prefer to scandalize someone or all of you saying that the cruelty against people (and their life at first!!) and the disruption of the material symbols of their past are **not justifiable**, I repeat **not justifiable**, but quite easy to understand in the present last frontier which is the ISIS fury. Rather than be silent. Rather than claim aloud for help against the barbarian of these destructions from the quite chairs of the top level management (sometimes forgetting about furthers contemporary crimes not so "mediatic").

The point is: who will win? Who will be in a majority or in a position of force to superimpose his/her values or defend those that the Past gave us?

Outstanding Value: **which will be the benchmark to define it?**

Only History will be able to witness the end of the conflict(s). But we can contribute in a positive way. We can save human life at first, as a value. The lack of value of (some) human lives is in fact at the basis of easy violence. Violence against Cultural Heritage is the way to give value to what could be not perceived as a value until it is destroyed. Unify killing of people at a Cultural site is the proof of it. At the same time is the proof of the lack of force of the message/ideology of the persons/groups who perpetrate the crime. Otherwise, they should not need such a show.

In such a situation, the main challenge and the most urgent task is to re-think (eventually re-confirming, but only after a wide-shared discussion, not only among specialists) the classification of Cultural Heritage according to the social **perception** of its message in different cultures and situations (not necessary critical). In this context also the behaviour of aggressive economy rather than different (geographical) thinkings, should be considered.

Differently, how can we propose World Heritage lists on a consensus basis? How to justify the conservation of cultural remains (and related expenses)? Why implement sophisticated tools with the help of new technologies to communicate a message that may be not understood? Why to invest resources for services if tourism is no more a need or possible?

These considerations are at the basis of the HERITY[1] approach, mainly related to the individuation of social consensus (or not) and the individual perception of the value of a cultural asset. Conservation, Communication and Services are necessarily affected by the first point. Also in "developed" Countries, the "enemy" is the doubt that it is worth to save cultural heritage instead of different options (e.g., building infrastructures). **Then, what to say in economies where people has no possibility to eat, to drink safe water, to live?**

A possible answer should be that, since pre-history, human beings are characterized by reasoning and acting according to their thoughts, which can be compared only with past experiences, not with future ones. So, having **the possibility to reason about our culture(s) at a global scale, eventually for changing it, should be considered among primary human rights**. This is possible only if we are put in the condition to know past events and their remains.

Please, contribute. If you trust your role.

---

[1] HERITY (from *Heritage* and *Quality*), International Organization for Quality Management at Cultural Sites which releases the HGES certification related to Value, Conservation, Communication and Services at a museum, archaeological site, library, archive or monument, was created exactly to fit the specific needs of Cultural Heritage care and valorization, with a special accent on social participation and consideration of local professionalities.

Landscape destruction and heritage mismanagement in Murujuga (Western Australia)

José Antonio GONZALEZ ZARANDONA
Alfred Deakin Institute of Citizenship and Globalization, Deakin University, Australia
antonio.g@deakin.edu.au

Abstract

Since the 1960s, the landscape of Murujuga, the largest archaeological site in the world, has been altered by the operation of mining companies, which have destroyed some of the unique petroglyphs found in open air. Different heritage management projects have been introduced to mitigate the impact that the mining companies have inflicted to the landscape. Whilst some of these projects have involved the local community, the majority have neglected and overlooked the social value of the local Indigenous community. It is thus necessary to review the methods so far implemented in Murujuga to envisage a solution to this conflict.

Keywords: *Murujuga, Iconoclasm, Cultural Heritage, Cultural Landscapes, Heritage Mismanagement*

Résumé

Depuis les années 1960, le paysage de Murujuga, le plus grand site archéologique dans le monde, a été modifié par le fonctionnement des sociétés minières, qui ont détruit certains des pétroglyphes uniques trouvés à l'air libre. Différentes projets de gestion de patrimoine ont été introduits pour atténuer l'impact que les sociétés minières ont infligé au paysage. Alors que certains de ces projets ont impliqué la communauté locale, la majorité a négligées et ignorées de la valeur sociale de la communauté indigène locale. Il est donc nécessaire de revoir les méthodes mises en œuvre dans la mesure Murujuga d'envisager une solution à ce conflit.

Mots clé: *Murujuga, Iconoclasme, Patrimoine Culturel, Paysage Culturel, Mauvais Gestion du Patrimoine*

Introduction

Located in the coastal Pilbara region of Western Australia, Murujuga, also known as the Burrup Peninsula, is part of the Dampier Archipelago (Western Australia). The area is said to host the world's largest concentration of petroglyphs with the number of motifs estimated to be in the order of one million (Vinnicombe 2002: 3; McDonald and Veth 2006: 149). Murujuga is an archaeological site, a sacred site, a national park and the operational site for at least a dozen of companies, which dwell on the mining business. Researchers estimate that 5-25 per cent of rock art on Murujuga has been removed or destroyed as a result of iron mining, industrial expansion and poor archaeological advice (Bednarik 2002: 30; 2006: 26; Donaldson 2009: 512). To this day there is no heritage management plan tailored to the needs of all the involved stakeholders: industry, archaeologists, Indigenous community and tourism. The future of Murujuga remains uncertain and only a few scholars are working towards its recognition as one of the truly magnificent World Heritage sites.

Heritage in the Burrup

Contemporary Aboriginal knowledge of Murujuga's petroglyphs was first appropriated by colonial history, and then reinstated in the industrial panorama of the 20th and 21st centuries (Mulvaney 2010: 135-136; González Zarandona 2012, 2015). Having knowledge reinstated by a culture other than those who made them, the petroglyphs carried the risk of being neglected and undervalued by the culture in which they are situated. Severed from Australian culture, they are considered a product of Aboriginal culture and a remnant of the past. Their significance is not particularly relevant for the prevailing ideology of multiculturalism in Australia. Seen from this perspective, the destruction of Aboriginal petroglyphs on Murujuga falls into the category of iconoclasm devised by Boris Groys

FIGURE 1. UNTIL THE NATURAL RESOURCES ARE EXHAUSTED, THE MINING INDUSTRY WILL NOT LEAVE MURUJUGA, CONTRIBUTING TO THE DESTRUCTION OF THE LANDSCAPE (PHOTO BY THE AUTHOR, OCTOBER 2012).

(2002: 283): an advancing force that destroys what "has become redundant, powerless, and void of inner meaning". Despite the destruction, Murujuga was admitted into the Australian National Heritage List in 2007, and declared a National Park in 2013.

But even if Murujuga has been legally recognised as cultural heritage, it continues to be neglected. This heritage recognition merely emphasised the line that separates postcolonised Aboriginal culture from neo-colonialist Australian culture. This division, in turn, has blocked the constitution of a common cultural heritage, creating instead a divergence that can still be witnessed today in regards to the conservation, evaluation and management of Aboriginal cultural heritage in Australia.

The other great cause of destruction and neglect on Murujuga and the difficulty in creating a unique heritage common to all Australians is the conflicting perceptions of the same piece of land; not to mention the power of whoever holds those perceptions. Whilst the Aboriginal community sees Murujuga as a collective territory of common management, unalienable, attached to history and local culture, non-Aboriginal people see it as a land that can be changed, transformed, sold and exploited (Fig. 1). Conflict thus arises from the imposition of a neocolonialist model of thinking on the management practices of a postcolonised group (Bonfil Batalla, 1993: 30-32), and there are several problems that derive from this circumstance.

Social value

The problem with being inclusive and pondering all values concerning a specific heritage place is how to choose the values that are most relevant. Either one value is more important than others, overriding the significance of the others, or all values are considered a "black box", where "all aspects of heritage value [are] collapsed into 'significance'" (Mason 2002: 8). Both positions are problematic and can be exclusive in their own way. An example of the former is how the archaeological discourse of heritage privileges the visual over other senses, disregarding the social value, for example. How contemporary Aboriginal people are forced to use certain concepts to describe how valuable their culture is for them is an example of the latter. Because the heritage system favours some values or meanings over others, heritage is understood either in terms of the past or the future, but cannot reflect traditional and contemporary values simultaneously (Byrne *et al.* 2001: 60-61; see also Tunbridge and Ashworth 1996; Carman 2002, 2005; Smith 2006; Cooper 2008). To overcome the problem, Aboriginal communities have had to develop a scientific vocabulary using foreign "accepted and well-defined categories of significance" to protect their most valuable places (McIntyre-Tamwoy 2004: 183). This is especially the case when they interchange *sacred* with *secular*, because it may be the only way in which a significant site can find meaning within the present heritage system and might otherwise, not be recognised and thus neglected.

For the Aboriginal community, social value is perhaps the most important value of Murujuga. This value "embraces the qualities for which a place has become a focus of spiritual, political, national or other cultural sentiment to a majority or minority group" (Australia ICOMOS 2000: 12).[1] The significance of the petroglyphs and the place for the local Aboriginal community is intangible and cannot be measured, explained or defined in terms of Western semiotic, iconographic or hermeneutic methodologies (*cf.* Johnston 1994). Their meaning is considered too sacred to be revealed, thus for the uninitiated they are empty symbols. With the creation of Aboriginal Corporations such as the Ngarluma Aboriginal Corporation, Yindjibarndi Aboriginal Corporation, and the Murujuga Aboriginal Corporation, the social value of the site is gradually being recognised. But it could be argued that Aboriginal people were forced to create corporations so that they could express their concerns about the destruction of their heritage from the perspective of the archaeological discourse of heritage.

In contrast, to the eyes of industry, social value is the least important value. On Murujuga, early settlers, industrial and archaeological surveys, and heritage assessments did not always consider this particular value. Because intangible values such as social values cannot be represented by an image or a number, it adds to the difficulty for some cultures to understand and recognise the value of a place that exists for a certain community or group. To complicate matters even more, Native Title rights (a social value, nonetheless) are only recognised if Aboriginal claimants can demonstrate that they have a continuous link to the area (Flood 2006: 245). In Murujuga, this is difficult because the Aboriginal groups who originally occupied the archipelago were annihilated as a result of colonialism, and the few survivors were forced to emigrate to nearby stations or seek refuge in missions (Gara 1983, 1984). The value that the natural resources have is considered more valuable than the Native Title rights that precede their discovery.

If social value is applied to the site, it should be equally applied to the whole local community, not only to the Aboriginal community. In other words, all of the social values attached to the site should be made visible. Of course, this might be controversial, but if we accept the premise that multiculturalism is the official ideology of Australia, then all interested parties (with their tangible and intangible values; Aboriginal and non-Aboriginal), need to be included in an inclusive heritage management plan. Otherwise, the site will be converted into an empty, un-interpreted, dispossessed site, that is nevertheless, full of meanings.

An assessment of Murujuga based on the *Burra Charter* would show the immense social value that the site has for the local Aboriginal community in terms of the spiritual and sacred values attached to the land and the rock art, as well as the social values it has for the local non-Aboriginal community. Thus, the people who have interpreted, valued, felt, lived and used the (heritage) site should also assess the social value in Murujuga (*cf.* Boyd 2012), considering not only the present but also the future and the past in terms of the sociocultural and economic values of this heritage site.

---

[1] Not surprisingly, the Heritage Council of Western Australia has not yet endorsed the Burra Charter as a guiding policy document for heritage management.

Thus, a balance between sociocultural values and economic values should follow (Mason 2002). I argue that the economic value of Murujuga should be included as a social value because different companies established in the area have contributed to the local Aboriginal community in different forms. This might be seen only as a small gesture that cannot compensate for the destruction caused, but it is also an extension of the extrinsic values that the local community have built over the years for the place they see as their workplace and home. For instance, Sam Walsh, Rio Tinto CEO, noted that his company has "been exporting iron ore from Dampier for more than forty years. During this time awareness and appreciation of the value of the rock art present in this area has grown immensely" (in Donaldson 2009). This value, new and based on economic value, should therefore be made known, because it represents the value that the industries have for the site. If the industries on Murujuga are not valuing the site for its Aboriginal cultural heritage, then we must understand how the site is of social value to them. It is imperative to understand the economic (social) value of the archipelago in terms of how much the local community actually gains from living in a sacred Aboriginal site.

Secular or sacred?

Another present problem is that Aboriginal heritage and non-Aboriginal heritage cannot be measured or valued in similar terms. Choosing to convert a sacred site like Murujuga into a secular one becomes problematic, because it's sacred reference for Aboriginal people distinguishes it from other sites and makes it important. Using the land as an industrial site in which people live and work desecrates it.

Having said that, I argue that removing the sacred reference from the rock art is a step towards considering the petroglyphs as universal (inclusive) heritage rather than a regional or national (exclusive) heritage. By being an exclusive site where Aboriginal people would perform ritual ceremonies, the site can be seen as sacred (the territory), whilst its international status as a masterpiece of human genius, shared by many cultural audiences, transforms it into a World Heritage Site (the map). Only then can the site be seen as a secular site charged with a religious past. This is why it is argued that heritage legislation is the best option to protect Murujuga in the absence of land rights (Veth *et al.*, 1993). Heritage is a more inclusive concept than art. As heritage, secular and sacred references to the petroglyphs can be combined, whereas with art historical or archaeological concepts, they must be one or the other (González Zarandona 2011, 2012, 2015).

Another advantage of turning a sacred site into a secular one is that it can be opened up to a larger, wider audience, and studied by many disciplines. A site like Murujuga can cross over to the threshold of science by losing some of its Aboriginality (its authenticity). It is argued that this action results in the loss of meaning at a local level (Taruvinga and Ndoro 2003: 4), but by being exclusive to the eye of science, the place loses its inclusiveness in the Aboriginal cosmogony. The prevailing heritage legislation presupposes that local meanings should be discarded, so that Murujuga gains other meanings. It is a matter of understanding heritage on multiple levels.

Levels of heritage

Heritage levels can be very problematic because including a site in one category may exclude it from another (Carman 2002: 11-12; *cf.* Gamboni 1997). Some assessments have been made to seek nomination of the site as World Heritage site, but to no avail (McDonald and Veth 2011; Anon. 2012). National Heritage since 2007, within the state of Western Australia Murujuga is recognised in terms of its natural resources rather than for the cultural values it possesses (Kuhlenbeck 2010). According to the state authorities, the site is an Aboriginal heritage site, but it is not considered sacred. But on a local level, the place is considered sacred because of its petroglyphs. As we have seen, the site is also important for non-Aboriginal employees working in the area, as it is the place in which they live and have built significant social relationships. In fact, non-Aboriginal stories attached to the site have already emerged.

This polysemy culminates in a semioclasm (the destruction of meaning), because national values and meanings are obliterating local Aboriginal values and meanings. What meanings and values should we then accept? Where does one jurisdiction end and another begin? According to the 1964 *Venice Charter*, one of the first heritage documents to have ever addressed this issue, "It is essential that the principles guiding the preservation and restoration of ancient buildings should be agreed and laid down on an international basis, with each country being responsible for applying the [Venice Charter] within the framework of its own culture and traditions" (http://www.s.org/charters/venice_e.pdf Consulted 14 Dec 2012).

This idea is still relevant because no international heritage law can override national heritage law, but it presupposes a myriad of meanings and values that are not clearly defined, and where different values and meanings overlap. Following a vertical jurisdiction, international or universal values may be more important than the rest, even though some universal values can be only understood at a local level. In contrast, in a horizontal scale of values all values are considered equally important and it is difficult to know which ones are the most important. In Murujuga we might visualise the overlapping of values as a group of spheres, each colliding with the others. The difficulty resides in knowing which one will eventually absorb the others due to its greater power. In the eventual case that the original values and meanings derived from Aboriginal contemporary attitudes towards Murujuga are considered the most important, the task and effort of evaluating the place in terms of the prevailing heritage system starts to reveal its futility. However, recognising the site as heritage at least provides a degree of signification.

Each country, culture and group has its own ways of evaluating whether an object, site or a tradition is to be considered heritage. It is only by the efforts of a wider community that an object, site or tradition is made fit for heritage consideration (Heyd 2005: 8).

Intangible values

Of all the values and meanings that Murujuga has, intangible ones are the most difficult to pinpoint. But if we cannot measure them, we can at least acknowledge them. Intangible cultural heritage can be divided into two groups. The first includes the customs and traditions that were practiced within their original and social context, but that due to colonialism have been lost together with their functions and meanings. No longer extant, they are symbols of aspects of culture. The second group encompasses all those customs and traditions that are still practiced within their natural and social context. These heritage practices are considered traditional and contemporary because they stem from a living culture that uses them to reaffirm identity. The culture of minority groups like Indigenous people around the world belongs to this second group (Yin 2006: npa). Both groups of intangible cultural heritage are currently present in Murujuga. The petroglyphs are tangible in form, whilst their content conforms to Yin's definition of intangible cultural heritage. Their content in some instances is not extant because it is kept secret, though still alive among the few Aboriginal descendants who know their meaning. The role of heritage officers on Murujuga is to facilitate the visibility of these intangible values, but they have failed considerably. We must ask if they have failed because they have simply not facilitated the values or because it cannot be done until the Aboriginal community agrees to allow them to be known.

Presentation or Conservation?

The ultimate question addressed by this chapter is how should we conserve or present a heritage site like Murujuga. On one hand, the economic growth of Australia is sustained by the mining industry and the companies working in WA. On the other hand, it has been asked:

> "What is the Burrup's rightful place in today's Australia? Is it a quarry or a sacred site and are the two things that different in our thoughts? Who should protect it, under what terms and how? [...] What value survives in such art when it is so fenced in and framed by industry, when its survival

is so artificial and fragmented in the landscape? Does the Burrup still live and have force as a religious and ritual site?"[2]

It is imperative to expose the immaterial and material values that the archipelago has. Both are important and both contribute to its greatness. But for the presentation factor, the material values are primordial, because people are attracted to material objects and when a caption states their significance, they feel rewarded. When they cannot see something, like the colonial settlers (agents of blindness), they become frustrated. In addition, tangible objects are credible because they can be seen and touched. They are evidence of ancient history and charged with authority. They "communicate in the absence of the communicator" (White 2003: 15).

But why should the petroglyphs be open to the public, if only one tenth of the 30,000 tourists who visit Woodside Visitor Centre every year wander through the rock "galleries"?[3] Should the value of potential tourism of the archipelago be discarded? It seems that to save the art from destruction, it is necessary to turn it into a commodity, by conveying part of its meaning. But the meaning of the petroglyphs will be then compromised because it should not be disclosed, for two reasons. This first is that Aboriginal tradition dictates that some images are not to be seen for cultural reasons. The second is that conveying the meaning would mean a considerable amount of tourists would visit a region that would not be able to host them. However, it seems that through public recognition the site could achieve a new status, and with it, protection, although Murujuga should not be converted into a theme park, as the Burrup Peninsula Conservation Reserve suggests (CALM 2003).

Furthermore, since the myriad of meanings, values and associations attached to the site are difficult to convey in a single report, it is necessary to start thinking about the future in terms of artworks, since archaeological assessments have undermined the power of the aesthetic value of the area. A management plan should then consider the place in terms of what it is, and not of what could be. In this sense, McDonald and Veth's definition of plan management is accurate: the plan should define "how to ascribe values to cultural materials so that these might be managed without their significance(s) being compromised" (McDonald and Veth 2005: 171). In other words, heritage and all its values, unlike its meanings, are not negotiable. But heritage assessments sometimes are undertaken, based on the value that the cultural material possesses. In the same manner that Hegel saw that to a corresponding form followed certain content, the values of heritage will be determined by a specific "owning institution" (Carman 2005: 60-61). In the case of Murujuga this is evident in their intangible and social values because they were not even considered in the management plans.

Carman claims (2005: 63) that the archaeological discourse of heritage sees archaeological remains as property and they are therefore treated as such. In Murujuga the industry has appropriated the site with the purpose to administer natural resources, strengthening the economic values derived from it. For this reason, the site will not be returned to the Aboriginal community until the deferred values (Carman 2005: 54) of the archaeological remains are put in use. This means that until the exploitation of the natural resources is not relinquished and the site is converted into a profitable cultural centre, Murujuga will be owned by the industry. Even though it is a national park and national heritage, the sole owner of it is the industry and that is precisely its most important value. Carman claims that the label of national heritage endows the state with prestige and authority (Carman 2005: 75-77), which in the case of Murujuga the prestige of the state would lie in protecting the site.

Although the comparison may be misleading, it is simply a matter of remembering how European governments are dealing with similar heritage sites that are open to the public, such as Altamira or Lascaux. I said misleading because the comparison does hold up if we think in terms of importance, not size. In other words, the archipelago needs to gain importance just as the European sites are invested

---

[2] www.theaustralian.com.au/news/culture-clash/story-e6frg8ox-1111119087923 (Accessed 5th April 2009).
[3] www.theaustralian.com.au/news/culture-clash/story-e6frg8ox-1111119087923 (Accessed 5th April 2009). See also ABC Radio National (2013), http://www.abc.net.au/radionational/programs/360/red-dirt-dreaming-part-two-the-pilbara/4538232

with significance. How can this be achieved? The publication of articles and reports is not enough, as they reveal the area's values, but not its meanings. A first step is to achieve cohesion and consider the site as a landscape filled with (rock) art galleries, rather than as fragmented archaeological sites. Rather than stating mere facts as the poor signs on site do, it is necessary to tell the story of the site.

A solution is to show the beauty of the art and the place. Aesthetics should play a greater role, because we are dealing with hundreds of thousands of works of art. People should travel to see the site because they find it beautiful and interesting, not because it hosts a mammoth industry hub. Murujuga should change from an industrial hub to a heritage site, combining its sacred features and its aesthetic qualities.

The problem in considering Murujuga as an artwork is that we need to bring aesthetics into the discussion. Where are aesthetics situated in regards to archaeological and Aboriginal heritage? Usually it is behind a set of criteria used to evaluate heritage. For example, the *Burra Charter* defines aesthetic values as that which "includes aspects of sensory perception for which criteria can and should be stated" (Australia ICOMOS 2000: 12). These criteria evaluate tangible aspects such as form, scale, colour, texture and material of the fabric, and also intangible aspects such as the smells and sounds attached to the place and its use.

When Aboriginal art is seen through the prism of aesthetics, we look for other elements such as subject matter, iconography and what it is telling us about another culture. In other words, we search for an answer that we do not seek in other art. The disciplines that have studied it include anthropology, archaeology and ethnography, but not often philosophy. Ryan argues that visual art is the best form to understand the governing principles of another culture because it is not as ephemeral as other types of art such as song and dance (Ryan 1995: 37). Ironically, the example of Aboriginal rock art on Murujuga shows us that rock art can be ephemeral through destruction.

García Canclini (2010: 110) goes even further when he states that the similarities between Western contemporary and non-Western art are striking, when the aesthetic experience in both realms is considered. This leads us to the problem of how we interpret the continuities, the coincidences and the discrepancies between what we consider ethnographic in the objects and what we value in what they do not tell us. García Canclini states that heritage professionals work with *eminence*, rather than with *imminence*; that which has already happened: goods that are deteriorated or at risk of disappearing. According to him, historians and archaeologists are moved by a negative imminence.

It is safer to assume that rock art is heritage as opposed to art. But according to anthropologist James Clifford (1991: 241), the best method to endow "cross-cultural value (moral and commercial) to a cultural production is to treat it as art." So if Murujuga is considered one of the most impressive clusters of art in the world, World Heritage status and a place in the Global History of Art may be easier to achieve. However, in Australia, Aboriginal sites are regarded as heritage sites and consequently, archaeological sites; but not as art.

Endowing the status of art to lines engraved onto rocks is difficult because we do not have the required information on the cultural framework of their makers. Heyd argues (2012: 288) that endowing the status of art to petroglyphs would be advisable, simply because we would take "seriously the creative activity of their makers." He may be correct, but it has also been argued that applying a "foreign" method such as aesthetics to a non-Western artefact to attract a large number of visitors can have dramatic consequences for the artefact and its meaning.[4] The question of whether we know the meaning of the rock art is still valid. If we agree that visual art "is a universal language that is open to all peoples to use and appreciate" (Ryan 1995: 37), then aesthetics can be used without resorting to the same misapprehension that it is a European concept (*cf.* Heyd 2012). The important thing to remember here is that there are different methods of evaluating a work of art from an aesthetic point

---

[4] Rambelli and Reinders (2007: 31) even claim that it amounts to semioclasm and iconoclasm.

of view. For instance, in Murujuga the space that the petroglyphs occupy needs to be considered, following Morphy's (1992: 10) definition of aesthetics, that properties of an object can be physical and non-material attributes of the object. Needless to say, Murujuga's rock art has both. Ultimately, if we wish to prevent more destruction in Murujuga, introducing "foreign" objects such as rock art to Western people can have the benefit of making them reflect on different views and different conceptions of the world (Morphy 1992: 7). This is what is commonly referred as cross-cultural aesthetics: incorporating the effects of an object on the senses of someone who is not familiar with that object, so that it is understood in the terms of the culture that produced it (Morphy 1992: 11).

For this reason, the conservation and presentation of petroglyphs is seemingly opposed: heritage on one side and art on the other. Aesthetics is framed by the traditional ways of preserving old places and the modern ways dictated by international organisations. It is argued that maintaining old traditions at Aboriginal sites as part of the conservation process can produce "overlapping spheres of knowledge and obligation" because each culture has a different way of relating to old places (Layton 1992: 59; Byrne et al., 2001: 63). Some cultures simply destroy them while others preserved them. Related to the concept of iconoclasm devised by Groys (2002: 283), destruction of a significant site is the product of an action that seeks progression or simply an interpretation (not to say justification) of a new regime that seeks to overturn the past and create a new beginning, e.g. the destruction of significant Islamic heritage sites in Mali in 2012 and the so-called Cultural Revolution in China (1966-1976). In any case, both actions are in most cases explicitly advertised as constructive actions. Is this not the situation that we encounter today between international, national, state, local and Aboriginal legislation in relation to Aboriginal and Australian heritage?

Conclusion

Conserving or presenting is still a challenge, because traditional ways of conserving rock art are in opposition with the global perspective of development, embodied by the companies established on Murujuga. Furthermore, latest developments in regard to the regulation of heritage laws have deregistered Murujuga as a sacred site, after the State Solicitor's Office in Western Australia advised the Western Australian Indigenous Affairs Minister, Peter Collier, that Murujuga is not a sacred site since "to be considered a sacred site, it must be demonstrated that it is devoted to a religious use rather than just a place subject to mythological story, song or belief" (Aboriginal Cultural Material Committee 2015). This of course relates to the different perceptions in which intangible heritage is valued from a Western perspective as analysed above.

Bibliography

ABORIGINAL CULTURAL MATERIAL COMMITTEE 2015. [Consult. 10 May 2015]. Available at URL: http://www.parliament.wa.gov.au/parliament/pquest.nsf/Parliament/pquest.nsf/SrchQON/D8659042187B109548257E0E000E60C3?opendocument

ANONYMOUS 2012. The Potential Outstanding Universal Value of the Dampier Archipelago Site and Threats to that Site. Canberra: Australian Heritage Council to the Minister for Sustainability, Environment, Water, Population and Communities. 79 p.

BEDNARIK, R. 2002. "The survival of the Murujuga (Burrup) petroglyphs." Rock Art Research. Vol. 19 (1), pp. 29-40.

BEDNARIK, R. 2006. Australian Apocalypse. The story of Australia's greatest cultural monument. Occasional AURA Publication 14, Australian Rock Art Research Association, Inc.: Melbourne.

BONFIL BATALLA, G. 1993. Nuestro patrimonio cultural: un laberinto de significados. In Florescano, E. ed. lit.- El patrimonio nacional de México, I. México: Fondo de Cultura Económica, p. 28-57.

BOYD, W. 2012. 'A Frame to Hang Clouds on': Cognitive Ownership, Landscape, and Heritage Management. In Skeates, R.; McDavid, C.; Carman, J., eds. lits.- The Oxford Handbook of Public Archaeology. Oxford: Oxford University Press, p. 172-198.

BYRNE, D.; BRAYSHAW, H.; IRELAND, T. 2001. Social significance. A discussion paper. Hurtsville NSW: NSW National Parks and Wildlife Service. 165 p.

CARMAN, J. 2002. Archaeology and Heritage. An Introduction. London, New York: Continuum. 242 p.

CARMAN, J. 2005. Against Cultural Property. Archaeology, Heritage and Ownership. London: Duckworth. 146 p.

CLIFFORD, J. 1991. Four Northwest Coast Museums: Travel Reflections. In Karp, I.; Lavine, S., eds. lits.- Exhibiting cultures: The poetics and politics of museum display. Washington, D.C.: Smithsonian Institution Press, p. 212-254.

CONSERVATION AND LAND MANAGEMENT 2003. Management Plan for the Burrup Peninsula Conservation Reserve. Department of Environment and Conservation. [Consult. 19 Jan 2011]. Available at URL: http://www.ont.dotag.wa.gov.au/B/burrup_and_maitland_industrial_estates.aspx; http://www.ont.dotag.wa.gov.au/_files/Burrup_Agreement.pdf; http://www.ont.dotag.wa.gov.au/_Files/burrup_draft.pdf

COOPER, M. 2008. This is not a Monument: Rhetorical Destruction and the Social Context of Cultural Resource Management. Public Archaeology. 7:1, p. 17-30.

DONALDSON, M. 2009. Burrup Rock Art. Ancient Aboriginal rock art of Burrup Peninsula and Dampier Archipelago. Western Australia: Wildrocks Publications. 516 p.

FLOOD, J. 2006. The Original Australians. Story of the Aboriginal People. Crows Nest, NSW: Allen & Unwin. 320 p.

GAMBONI, D. 1997. The Destruction of Art. Iconoclasm and Vandalism since the French Revolution. New Haven, London: Yale University Press. 416 p.

GARA, T. J. 1983. The Flying Foam Massacre: an incident on the North-West Frontier, Western Australia. In Smith, M. ed. lits.- Archaeology at ANZAAS 1983. Perth: Anthropology Department Western Australian Museum, p. 86-94.

GARA. T. J. 1984. The Aborigines of the Dampier Archipelago: an ethnohistory of the Yaburarra. Perth: Western Australia Museum, npa.

GARCÍA CANCLINI, N. 2010. La sociedad sin relato. Antropología y estética de la inminencia. Buenos Aires, Madrid: Katz Editores, p. 264.

GONZÁLEZ ZARANDONA, J. A. 2011. The Destruction of Heritage: Rock Art in the Burrup Peninsula. The International Journal of the Humanities. 9:1, p. 325-342.

GONZÁLEZ ZARANDONA, J. A. 2012. How Many Times Can the Same Image Change? The History of the Image in Murujuga. The International Journal of the Image. 2:4, p. 95-109.

GONZÁLEZ ZARANDONA, J. A. 2015. Towards a Theory of Landscape Iconoclasm. Cambridge Archaeological Journal. 25:2, p. 461-475.

GROYS, B. 2002. Iconoclasm as an Artistic Device. Iconoclastic Strategies in Film. In Latour, B.; Weibel, P., eds. lits.- Iconoclash. Beyond the Image Wars in Science, Religion and Art. Boston: MIT Press, p. 286-295.

HEYD, T. 2005. Aesthetics and Rock Art: An Introduction. In Heyd, T.; Clegg, J., eds. lits.- Aesthetics and Rock Art. London: Ashgate, pp. 2-17.

HEYD, T. 2012. Rock "Art" and Art: Why Aesthetics Should Matter. In McDonald, J.; Veth, P., eds. lits.- A Companion to Rock Art. Oxford, Malden: Wiley-Blackwell, p. 276-293.

JOHNSTON, C. 1994. What is Social Value? Australian Heritage Commission [online]. Canberra. [Consult. 19 Jan 2011]. Available at URL: http://www.teachingheritage.nsw.edu.au.

KUHLENBECK, B. 2010. Re-Writing Spatiality: The Production of Space in the Pilbara Region in Western Australia. Berlin: Lit Verlag AL, 300 p.

LAYTON, R. 1992. Australian rock art: a new synthesis. Cambridge: Cambridge University Press, 304 p.

MASON, R. 2002. Assessing Values in Conservation Planning: Methodological Issues and Choices. In de la Torre, M. Assessing the Values of Cultural Heritage. Research Report. Los Angeles: The Getty Conservation Institute, p. 5-30.

MCDONALD, J.; VETH, P. 2005. Desktop assessment of Scientific Values for Indigenous Cultural Heritage on the Dampier Archipelago, Western Australia. Canberra: Jo McDonald Cultural Heritage Management Pty Ltd. 225 p. Report.

McDonald, J.; Veth, P. 2006. A study of the distribution of rock art and stone structures on the Dampier Archipelago. Canberra: Jo McDonald Cultural Heritage Management Pty Ltd. 195 p. Report.

McDonald, J.; Veth, P. 2011. Study of the Outstanding Universal Values of the Dampier Archipelago, Western Australia. 214 p. Report.

McIntyre-Tamwoy, S. 2004. Places people value: Social significance and cultural exchange in post-invasion Australia. In Harrison, R.; Williamson, C., eds. lits.- *After Captain Cook: The archaeology of the recent indigenous past in Australia*. Walnut Creek, CA: Altamira Press, p. 171-190. (Indigenous Archaeologies Series).

Mulvaney, K. 2010. Murujuga Marni – Dampier Petroglyphs. Shadows in the landscape. Echoes across time. Unpublished PhD thesis. University of New England.

Morphy, H. 1992. Aesthetics in a Cross-Cultural Perspective: Some Reflections on Native American Baskery. JASO. 23:1, p. 1-16.

Rambelli, F.; Reinders. E. 2007. What does iconoclasm create? What does preservation destroy? Reflections on iconoclasm in East Asia. In Boldrick, S.; Clay, R., eds. lits.- Iconoclasm: Contested Objects, Contested Terms. England, USA: Ashgate, p. 15-34.

Ryan, J. 1995. The raw and the cooked: the aesthetic principle in Aboriginal art. Art Bulletin of Victoria. 36, p. 37-50.

Smith, L. 2006. The Uses of Heritage. Abingdon: Routledge. 368 p.

Taruvinga, P.; Ndoro, W. 2003. The vandalism of the Domboshava rock painting site, Zimbabwe: Some reflections on approaches to heritage management. In Stanley-Price, N., ed. lit.- Conservation and Management of Archaeological Sites. 6:1, p. 3-10.

The Burra Charter 2000. Burwood VIC: Australia ICOMOS. 12 p. The Australia ICOMOS Charter for Places of Cultural Significance.

Tunbridge, J. E.; Ashworth, G. J. 1996. Dissonant Heritage: The Management of the Past as a Resource in Conflict. Chichester: Wiley. 299 p.

Veth, P.; Bradshaw, E.; Gara, T.; Haydock, P.; Hall, N.; Kendrick, P. 1993. Burrup Peninsula. Aboriginal Heritage Project. Perth: Department of Conservation and Land Management. 256 p. Report.

Vinnicombe, P. 2002. Petroglyphs of the Dampier Archipelago: background to development and descriptive analysis. Rock Art Research. 19. p. 3-27.

White, R. 2003. *Prehistoric art: the symbolic journey of humankind*. New York: Harry Abrams. 240 p.

Yin, T. 2006. Museum and the Safeguarding of Intangible Cultural Heritage. *The Ethic Arts*. 6, npa.

Media strategies observed in the Portuguese press to save Vila Nova de Foz Côa engravings. A case study on socialization of the archaeological heritage

Cinta S. BELLMUNT
journalist, archeologist and responsible for Communication at the IPHES
(Institut Català de Paleoecologia Humana i Evolució Social)

Abstract

Several unusual factors made possible the conservation of Foz Côa's rock art engraved. Luckily, the capacity of a group of researchers, the archaeologists, managed to mobilize different powers and build different international alliances. Furthermore, a great social dynamic occurred. The Portuguese society, in general, was mobilized. The case became a national problem and the construction of a hydroelectric power station and a reservoir that could have submerged the archaeological heritage were stopped definitely. The media impact was very important, but it wasn't the unique reason. In this research, we review the different factors involved and the strategies of communication used to save the engravings.

Keywords: *Media, strategies of communication, archaeological heritage, socialization*

Résumé

Plusieurs facteurs inhabituels ont rendu possible la conservation des gravures rupestres de Foz Côa. Heureusement, la capacité d'un groupe de chercheurs, les archéologues, a réussi à mobiliser différents pouvoirs et construire différentes alliances internationales. En outre, une grande dynamique sociale s'est développée. La société portugaise, en général, a été mobilisée. Le cas est devenu un problème national et la construction d'une centrale électrique hydroélectrique et d'un réservoir qui pourrait avoir submergé l'héritage archéologique ont été arrêtés définitivement. L'impact des médias a été très important, mais ce n'a pas été l'unique raison. Dans ce travail nous considérons les différents facteurs impliqués et les stratégies de communication utilisées pour sauver les gravures.

Mots clés: *Médias, stratégies de communication, héritage archéologique, socialisation*

Introduction

In 1994 the alarm was raised. The water level of the river Côa lowered and some engravings were discovered. An archaeologist reported the finding to the mass media. She considered these engravings were an exceptional discovery. The building of a hydroelectric power station and a reservoir could endanger this heritage.

Soon an international campaign was started to denounce the matter. The civil society and the mass media gave their full support to the campaign. The principal argument was the exceptional value of the engravings and it was demanded to halt the construction and save this heritage.

The goal of this research was to analyze the communications strategies of the mass media to save the engravings. This question was very important but there were other factors which I also studied. For example, how this issue became a matter of state and the reasons behind the social movement. It was the only time that the construction of a reservoir was stopped and an archaeological park was built instead.

Foz Côa site

The case I am going to introduce took place in Vila Nova de Foz Côa in the North East of Portugal near Oporto, on the banks of the Duero and Côa rivers, 194 km from Oporto, 380 km from Lisbon,

FIGURE 1. GEOGRAPHICAL LOCATION.

both cities in Portugal, and 182 km from Salamanca, in Spain. It belongs to the District da Guarda, North Region and subregion of the Duero. Together with Meda and Pinhel it shares the traces of prehistoric rock art which are currently included in the Archaeological Park of the Valley of Côa. The site is the largest and most important collection of open-air rock art in the world. The engravings are carved in schist rock. It is composed of more than 40 sites along the last 17 kilometers of the river Côa before its confluence with the Duero. They are of an extraordinary beauty. They belong to the Upper Paleolithic (25,000 years ago).

In 1997, there were declared a National Monument of Portugal and, one year later, Patrimony of the Humanity although some more modern engravings realized in different periods of the prehistory (Neolithic, Iron Age …) were discovered in that area.

Until their discovery it was thought that artistic creations of this importance were only

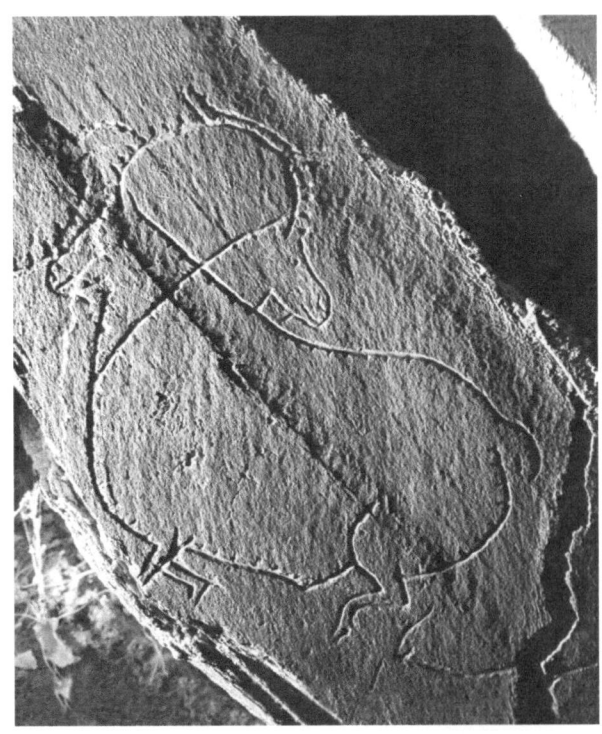

FIGURE 2. MOST OF THE FIGURES CRAVED IN FOZ CÔA REPRESENT ANIMALS, MAINLY HORSES, AUROCHS, CERVIDS AND GOATS.

carried out inside caves. However, Foz Côa is a huge set of thousands of figures outdoors realized on blocks of different pieces of schist spread throughout the territory. That was breaking away from the idea that prehistoric communities only recreated art in closed places; moreover, archaeological finds are normally of small dimensions, but here we are before an enormous collection. The more it is being investigated, the more it brings forward proof that it is the largest outdoors set in the world of these characteristics and of this period.

Most of the figures craved in Foz Côa represent animals, mainly horses, aurochs, cervids and goats, many of which are superposed, although it is not known yet why it is like that. Also there is some human representation and some others related to signs.

Materials analyzed

I analyzed different materials and interviewed some journalists and archaeologists involved in the case.

The Bibliography about this issue is very limited and was reviewed but I have also consulted books regarding the situation of Portugal in the middle of the nineties of last century, when the facts took place, in order to discover factors that could play in favor of saving the rock art of Foz Côa. I have also consulted various publications related to the sociology of mass communication, the effects of the mass media and the communication strategies.

I mainly studied news published in Portuguese newspapers and other selected news from important foreign newspapers from November 1994 to December 1995. A total of 500 news articles were read among which 150 were analyzed in depth.

Moreover, I interviewed 13 people about this case: archaeologists (4), university professors (2), journalists (3), and residents in Foz Côa (3), as well as the director of the Archaeological Park of the Côa Valley (1).

I also carried out a selection of news related to that same period from important foreign newspapers (20), as well as the front page-coverage of the weekly *Expresso*, 5; Letters to the international authorities, 15, and Press releases, 10.

Finally, I studied the social, political and cultural context. When the conflict of Foz Côa explodes, in November 1994, the Portuguese Republic (AR) was governed by the Democratic Social Party (PSD), with Aníbal Antonio Cavaco Silva as prime minister, being replaced in the position by António Manuel of Oliveira Guterres on October 28 1995 when the Socialist party won the elections. In that period, the president of the AR was Mário Soares.

These are the years when Portugal is adopting the slogan "think globally and act locally". Namely as we value our own cultural identity, we must also think more in the long term and beyond our borders, at planetary scale.

In turn, Portugal aspires to be a country with proper voice in the frame of the European Union, as well as to modernize, in a society who still drags some tendency of provincialism. It is, then, in a process of changing, of conquering new values and overcoming the heredity of the "salazarista" dictatorship that the country was looking for new openings in its international relations. In this sense, cultural elements based on the tradition, history and the patrimony are decisive.

Methods

The objective was to demonstrate Laswell's paradigm: *"Who says What to Whom in What Channel with What Effect"*. At the same time I was also interested in observing the evolution of the case: who takes prominence, the values involved and their evolution, who defends what, and so on. For this reason, I analyzed the information by means of both Quantitative and Qualitative Techniques.

Regarding Quantitative techniques I used content analysis, applied basically to a hundred and fifty articles from Portuguese newspapers, stratified non-random sampling of 500 news items and I applied the key variables as selection criteria. This was done with non-random stratified sampling of the population or the mentioned universe that is to say, the set of reference in which the observations are realized. This type of sampling consists of the previous division of the population of study in groups or classes that are supposed to be homogeneous with regard to the characteristic to be studied.

The printed mass media with more impact were taken into account. They were those which were then published every day in Portugal, with the exception of the general information weekly paper *Expresso*, that I considered because they sent a professional to follow the topic and it was a very influential publication, as well as *O Independente*, which, at that time, was fast-growing, although it does not exist anymore. The daily offer consisted of various newspapers, either morning ones or even some evening publications, but out of the analyzed sample those which had more presence, because of their monitoring of the topic of Foz Côa were: *Público, O Independente, O comércio do Porto, Correio du Manha, O Arrais, Jornal de Noticias* and *Diario de Notícias*; these two last ones are between the most widely read newspapers.

I also used Qualitative Techniques, basically interviews with relevant actors: scientists, journalists, university teachers, inhabitants of the town and agents of the park. The goal was to contrast the sources of information in depth and to have more points of view. The three journalists I interviewed were: Manuel Carvalho, who in 1994 was an editor of the *Diario Público* and was the first one to publish the facts; Valentina Marcelino, writer of the weekly paper *Expresso* who monitored the case closely and Pedro Garcías, editor of the *Público*, who often picked up the story as well.

I also talked to the following archaeologists: Robekt Bednarik, person in charge of the dating of the rock engravings entitled by the EDP, the company that was constructing the hydroelectric power station, and that was granting them a much more recent age to the one finally considered; Jean Clottes, who certified that the engravings were Paleolithic and were 20,000 years old, and who, at that time, was the president of the International Committee of Rock Art (ICOMOS – UNESCO); Emmanuel Anatti, specialist in world rock art, who was some of the experts invited to give their opinion about the characteristics of the engravings, certifying their value together with Clottes and Antonio Beltrán; and António Martinho Baptista, former director of the National Center of Rock Art (1997-2007) and who was invited by the government in 1994 to study the engravings and to verify their importance and chronology.

As for sociologists I took into account Maria Eduarda Gonçalves, author of the book *O caso de Foz Côa: Um laboratorio de análise sociopolítica*, and José Luis García, teacher at the Institute of Social Sciences of the University of Lisbon, who has written some articles about Foz Côa.

From the Archaeological Park Vilanova de Foz Côa I spoke with Alexandra Cerveira Pinto, who was the director in 2004.

As for the businesses in town I talked with: Isaura Aguilar, director of the "Casa Vermelha", an ancient country-house where it is possible to spend the night.

As for the neighbors of Foz Côa, José Manuel da Costa Ribeiro who was, at that time, president of the managing council of the Secondary School of Vila Nova de Foz Côa, and Adriano Ferreira, pensioner and discoverer of some engravings.

Moreover, I collected and studied weeklies, press releases and letters, International newspapers and I carried out interviews.

FIGURE 3. BIG CAMP IN FOZ CÔA.

To obtain quantifiable information I calculated different variables. From each news item I collected the following data: date of publication, name of the newspaper and headline. I also took into account other complementary information such as page, front-page, back page, presence of photography, authorship, extension, headline, secondary agent, subtitle, abstract, type and day of the week as well as key data: such as Focus, Main agent and Argument.

Results

With this material I observed different key moments. One of them was in December 1994 when international organizations sent letters to Mario Soares, the Portuguese President at that time. Another, in the same year, was when the economic interests were in conflict with the archaeological interests, because it was an extraordinary discovery. The scientific community soon realized the significance of the discovery and finally UNESCO recognized the exceptional value of the engravings. From then on, Foz Côa was in the international press.

In 1995, there were key moments too. In March a big camp was mainly organized by students and they demonstrated that "engravings-mania" was born. They gave Soares a manifesto and were playing a major role. At the same time, Mário Soares visited the engravings and agreed that it was necessary to preserve them. This same month *The Times* published an editorial.

There was a delicate moment when dating process showed that the engravings were more recent than it was thought. The results of this process put the date of the engravings in doubt. In July a "war" broke out among the archaeologists about the dating results. In September, the reservoir/engravings dichotomy was to be decided by the Parliament. In October there was a change of Government. Finally, in November the prime minister announced the construction work was to be stopped. There were protests by the inhabitants of Foz Coa, because they were worried about jobs and income. For

FIGURE 4. MÁRIO SOARES IN FOZ CÔA WHIT STUDENTS.

this reason, in December the authorities promised a great plan to promote the region of Foz Côa; the idea was to make the economic interests compatible with heritage conservation.

Discussion of the results

I observed some relevant data in the information. For example, journalists were quick to take an interest; in one month it was the most published news item (28%). The archaeologists began explaining to the public the scientific and cultural importance of the discovery. Their approach was didactic and the journalists quickly incorporated this into their Agenda-setting.

A slogan became popular: "The engravings don't know how to swim" and the engravings explain Prehistory in images. The popular argument to defend the preservation of the engravings was: "Foz Côa is the largest collection of open-air rock art in the world".

The agenda-setting focused on the "war" between scientists. There was great political, public and scientific controversy. The protest movement had the support of all Scientists and UNESCO.

Soon the "war" between institutions and archaeologists became popular in journalists' agenda-setting. All along the controversy an argument prevailed: The biggest collection of open-air rock art in the world. New discoveries appear continuously.

At the same time, EDP (the company that was promoting the construction of the hydroelectric power station) and IPPAR (organism that was managing the archaeological patrimony in Portugal) kept quiet or only spoke a little. They hid information and were under suspicion.

A political, public and scientific controversy was then generated. The mass media gave importance to tensions and conflict, and the civil society (Foz Côa's school, intellectuals…) started actions. The engravings became the talking point for village society and beyond, adopting an almost mythical status. Public opinion was formed and the conflict became a state problem.

Journalism was not objective! From the first moment the mass media, and especially some professionals, were in favor of saving the engravings.

It was the electoral year. The socialist party used Foz Côa as an electoral weapon: if they were in power they would stop the reservoir. Once the conflict was solved, the local inhabitants had great expectations for the archaeological park. When the Archaeological Park of Valle de Côa (PAVC) was opened there was some disappointment, because the park had a limited number of visits. There were access difficulties. It was not easy to visit the park. The village doesn't have the necessary infrastructures to receive visitors. Currently it is not very interesting for the mass media. And unlike those teams the research is poor.

But, the engravings were saved and work is being done to improve these social difficulties seeking new models to manage the heritage, like in Atapuerca (Spain) or Tautavel (France).

Conclusions

The following are some of the factors that helped reach a positive solution for the case: increased political, social and cultural awareness; the didactic explanations of the archaeologists, the sensitivity of the mass media, Mário Soares had political courage; teachers understood the pedagogical value of the heritage, it was the start of a dynamic of sensitivity to archaeology. Today, the Foz Côa engravings are an archaeological park and World Heritage.

Also, what have we learnt from Foz Côa? Well, the actors who don't communicate lose relevance. It is necessary to work more on socialization and to combine economic and cultural interests. Journalism can be partial but must always be honest. The complicity between archaeologists and journalists is good for the socialization of science.

Regarding this complicity with the media and considering what we have learned from Foz Côa, as a consequence of that study, we implemented new communicative strategies in our own institution: the Institut Català de Paleoecologia Humana i Evolució Social (IPHES) carries out various communications actions concerning the archaeological heritage we are researching. We have 6 blogs organized by language and target audience. Our news is written didactically. We are present in the social networks: Facebook, twitter, YouTube, Linkedin… and we have thousands of followers. We receive dozens of comments and we reply to all. We have our own spaces in the media: on the radio, on TV, in newspapers and on digital portals.

All of this has made the IPHES a benchmark for communication for other research centres across the world. Our experience has been published in books. We hold talks, provide training courses… And we have received awards.

Bibliography

AA.VV. 1998. Portugal na transição do milenio. Colóquio internacional. Lisboa, Fim de século.
AA.VV. 2007. Cidadania. Uma visão para Portugal. Lisboa, Gradiva.
ALBERTO, Rafael 2006. Estrategias de comunicación. Barcelona, Ariel Comunicación.
BARTHES, R., ELEMENTOS DE SEMIOLOGÍA 1971. Madrid, Alberto Corazón Editor.
BRYANT, J. y ZILLMANN, D. (compiladores) 1996. Los efectos de los medios de comunicación Barcelona, Paidós.
CARDOSO, R. (coordinador) 2007. Turismo Científico em Portugal. Lisboa, Assírio & Alvim.
CASETTI, F. *et al*. 1999. Análisis de la televisión. Barcelona, Paidós.
CHOMSKY, N. *et al*. 1995. Los guardianes de la libertad. Barcelona, Grijalbo Mondadori.
CHOMSKY N. *et al*. 2007. Cómo nos venden la moto. Barcelona, Icaria.
ECHEVERRÍA, J. 1999. Introducción a la metodología de la ciencia. La filosofia de la ciencia en el siglo XX. Colección Teorema. Madrid, Ediciones Cátedra, S. A.

FREIRE, A. et al. 2007. Eleições e Cultura Política. Impremsa de Ciências Sociais, Lisboa.
GIL, José 2007. Portugal, hoje. Lisboa, Relógio d'Água.
GONÇALVES, M. E. et al. 2001. O caso de Foz Côa: Um laboratorio de análise sociopolítica. Lisboa, Ediçoes 70.
GUBERN, R. 1987. La mirada opulenta. Barcelona, Editorial Gustavo Gili.
HABERMAS, J. 2001. Teoria de la acción comunicativa, I y II. Madrid, Taurus.
LIPPMANN, Walter 2003. La opinión pública. Madrid, Langre.
LOZANO, J. et al. 1999. Análisis del discurso. Madrid, Cátedra.
MACHUCA, G. 2006. El periodismo de investigación y la teoría crítica de la ciencia de Martín, Manuel (2007). Teoría de la comunicación. Madrid, Mc Graw Hill.
MARTINO, A. 1999. No tempo sem tempo. A arte dos caçadores paleolíticos do Vale do Côa. Albums do P.A.V.C. Vila Nova de Foz Côa.
MONTEIRO, M. et al. 1994. Viva Portugal. Uma nova ieaia da Europa. Lisboa, Publicações Europa – América.
MORAGAS, M. de 1986. Semiótica y comunicación de masas. Barcelona, Ediciones Península.
MORAGAS, M. de (ed.) 1985. Sociología de la Comunicación de masas. Barcelona, Editorial Gustavo Gili.
MORAGAS, M. de 1981. Teorías de la Comunicación. Barcelona, Editorial Gustavo Gili.
MOUNIN, G. 1971. Saussure. Presentación y textos. Barcelona, Editorial Anagrama.
POPPER, K. R. 1985. La lógica de la investigación científica. Estructura y función: el porvenir actual de la ciencia. Madrid, Editorial Tecnos, S. A. 7ª.
RODRIGO, M. 1989. La construcción de la noticia. Barcelona, Paidós.
URSUA, N. 1933. Cerebro y conocimiento: un enfoque evolucionista. Nueva Ciencia, 10. Barcelona, Editorial Anthropos.
VEIGA, O. da 1985. Portugal, pré-histórico. Seu enquadramento no Mediterrâneo. Lisboa, 1985.
VILCHES, L. 1987. Teoría de la imagen periodística. Barcelona, Ediciones Paidós.
WIMMER, R. D. et al. 1996. La investigación científica de los medios de comunicación. Barcelona, Bosch.
WOLF, Mauro 1992. Els efectes socials dels mitjans de comunicación de masses. Editorial Pòrtic.

Archaeological research and applied arts for Public Archaeology in a Final Bronze Age hilltop walled station of Castelo Velho da Zimbreira (Mação-Portugal)

Davide DELFINO
Instituto Terra e Memória (I.T.M.-Mação); Câmara Municipal de Abrantes
(Project M.I.A.A.); "Quaternary and Prehistory" Group of Geosciences Center (CGe-U.C.).
Largo Infante D. Henrique, 6120-750, Mação, Portugal
davdelfino@gmail.com

Dragos GHEORGHIU
Doctoral School, National University of Arts; 19 Budisteanu, Bucharest, Romania;
Instituto Terra e Memória (I.T.M.-Mação), Portugal
gheorghiu_dragos@yahoo.com

Livia STEFAN
University Politechnica of Bucharest, 313 Splaiul Independentei, Bucharest, Romania;
Institute for Computers Bucharest (ITC SA), Bucharest, Romania
livia.stefan@itc.ro

Abstract

Since 2010 the Land and Memory Institute and Museum of Prehistoric Art have been conducting ongoing research on the mechanisms of occupation of the territory and settlement dynamics in the Final Bronze Age/ Iron Age in the Mação Council (Central Portugal), with a specific focus on the Castelo da Zimbreira hilltop walled station and its relation with the landscape. The initial 2010 collaboration with the National University of Arts, Bucharest which produced a land art simulating the two wall/terrace lines of the settlement, was consolidated in 2013 through additional collaborative work within the framework of the Time Maps project and focused on public archaeology and Virtual Reality applications in archaeology.

Keywords: *hilltop site, Final Bronze Age, landscape, Public Archaeology, 3D reconstructions*

Résumé

Depuis 2010 l'Institut Terre et Mémoire et le Musée d'Art Préhistorique de Mação sont en train d'effectuer des recherches portant sur les mécanismes d'occupation du territoire et les dynamiques de peuplement, durant la période de l'Âge de Bronze Final/ Première Age du Fer dans le commune de Mação (Portugal Central). La recherche a été axée surtout sur le poste fortifié de Castelo Velho da Zimbreira et sur sa relation avec le paysage. La collaboration initiale (en 2010) avec l'Université Nationale des Arts de Bucarest, qui a réalisé une création de Land Art simulant les deux lignes de la muraille terrassée du site, a été poursuivie et solidifiée en 2013 avec des initiatives additionnelles pour valoriser le site dans le cadre du projet Time Maps, ainsi que avec l'aide de l'archéologie publique et des applications de Réalité Virtuelle.

Mots clés: *Station d'hauteur, Age du Bronze Final, territoire, Archéologie Publique, reconstructions 3D*

1. Introduction

Research on inhabited dynamics and landscape strategy occupation in the Final Bronze Age/Iron Age (XII-VII/VI cent BC) in the Portuguese Middle Tagus Valley has been ongoing since 2011 aiming to clarify what was the contribution of the substrate indigenous to the Final Bronze Age and what could be attributed to the dynamics initiated by contact with the Mediterranean world, starting from the IX/VIII cent BC (Vilaça, Arruda 2004; Arruda 2005; Delfino 2012). Focused in the council of Abrantes and Mação, the research has produced results (Delfino *et al.*, 2014) indicating the occurrence of a phenomenon of fortifications development (*incastellamento*) in the second part of the Final Bronze Age (X-VIII cent. BC) and linked in some parts of the territory surveyed to alluvial gold resources and the presence of ground waters. The paradigmatic site, which has been almost completely investigated, is Castelo Velho da Zimbreira (Parish of Envendos, Council of Mação). In order to sensitize the local population, students, tourists and scholars to this archaeological monument and to the historical dynamics linked to it, various approaches have been considered, each designed for a specific target audience. The issues encountered, requiring resolution are as follows: 1) lack of striking/monumental features of the archaeological site; 2) low population density and remoteness of the region concerned; 3) lack of adequate financing resources; 4) lack of visually conspicuous archaeological materials found.

2. Archaeological data

The archaeological monument of Castelo Velho da Zimbreira consists of two known terracing walls (with the possibility of a, yet unidentified, third wall) surrounding an area of about 8463 m² (0.84 hectares), set on a hill with panoramic 360° views over a vast territory. The settlement is part of a series of similar, fortified hilltop settlements, dating from the same Final Bronze Age period, all set at strategic points along a quartz belt that defines a specific territory (Fig. 1). Fieldwork carried out in 2011, 2012 and 2013 has investigated much of the external line of dry stone wall (wall 2): in the absence of any palaeosoil or other structure linked to the settlement, the area near the wall has been interpreted as a passage area, created by carving the rock to create the foundation of the wall (and using the stone thus obtained to build the wall in a dry stone technique); the extremities of

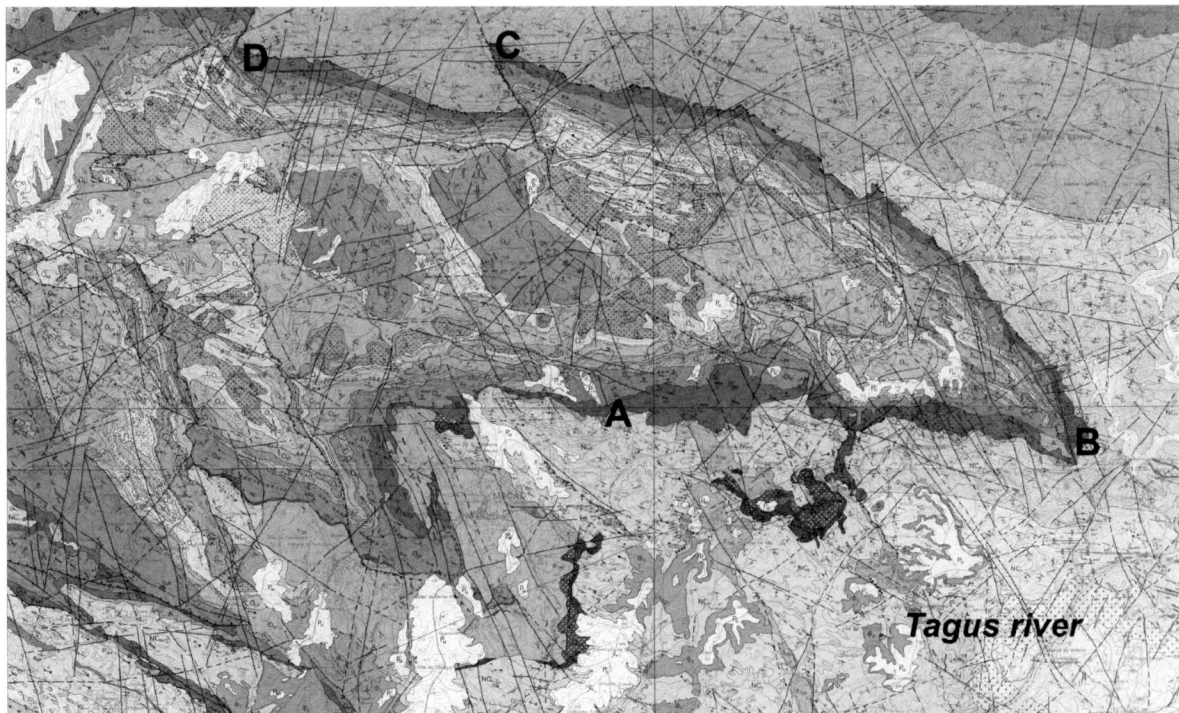

FIGURE 1. SYSTEM OF TERRITORY SETTLEMENT IN THE FINAL BRONZE AGE IN THE COUNCIL OF MAÇÃO: A- HILL TOP WALLED SETTLEMENT OF CASTELO VELHO DA ZIMBREIRA (MAÇÃO PARISH); B- HILL TOP WALLED STATION OF CASTELO VELHO DA ZIMBREIRA (ENVENDOS PARISH); C- HILL TOP WALLED STATION OF CASTRO DO SANTO (CARVOEIRO PARISH); D- HILL TOP WALLED STATION OF CASTRO DE AMÊNDOA (AMÊNDOA PARISH).

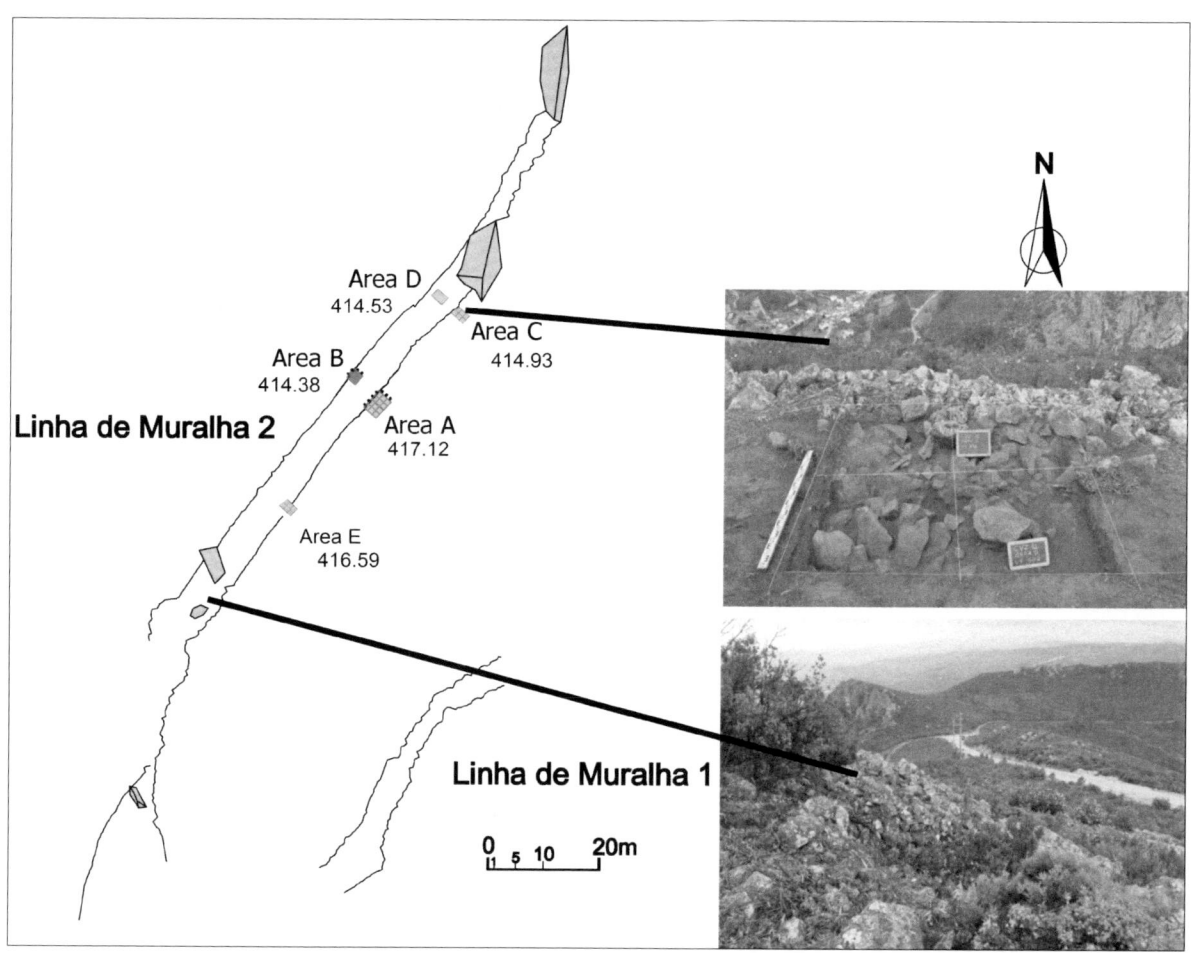

FIGURE 2. HILL TOP WALLED STATION OF CASTELO VELHO DA ZIMBREIRA: THE WALL 2 WITH INSTALLATION OF FIELDWORK SQUARES AND PICTURES OF THE TWO PLATFORMS AT THE EXTREMITIES OF THE WALL (BACKGROUND PLANT BY PEDRO CURA).

wall 2 lean following the natural quartz outcrops of the mountain side where they broadens into two massive platforms (*atalaias*) probably aimed at control of the territory (Fig. 2). The archaeological finds are represented by 600 pottery fragments, all contained in two colluvial layers originating from higher altitudes and whose downward flow was stopped by the wall (Fig. 3): some fragments display careened shapes, or burnished surfaces, or surfaces with burnished decorations, therefore dating broadly from the Final Bronze Age. Situated below the building stones of wall 2 and above the bedrock (i.e. the foundation of the wall), a completely carbonaceous and sterile layer was found, dated with AMS from the VIII-VII century BC.[1]

The walled station is situated on a panoramic hilltop, a position corresponding to one of the two fractures along the quartzite belt, both of which (during their formation) became the origin of several water sources as natural entrance ways in the water rich territory inside the belt; as a result the position of the Castelo Velho da Zimbreira is very strategic.

Three other walled sites can be found on the hilltop, along the quartzite belt: Castelo Velho do Caratão, dating from the Final Bronze Age this settlement has been explored in 1946, 1983 and 1984 (Horta

---

[1] Absolute date is BETA 379735-2590±30 BP- cal. 2 sigma 805-770 BC, but considering the margin of error of radiocarbon to I millennium BC, is considerable as VIII-VII cent. BC.

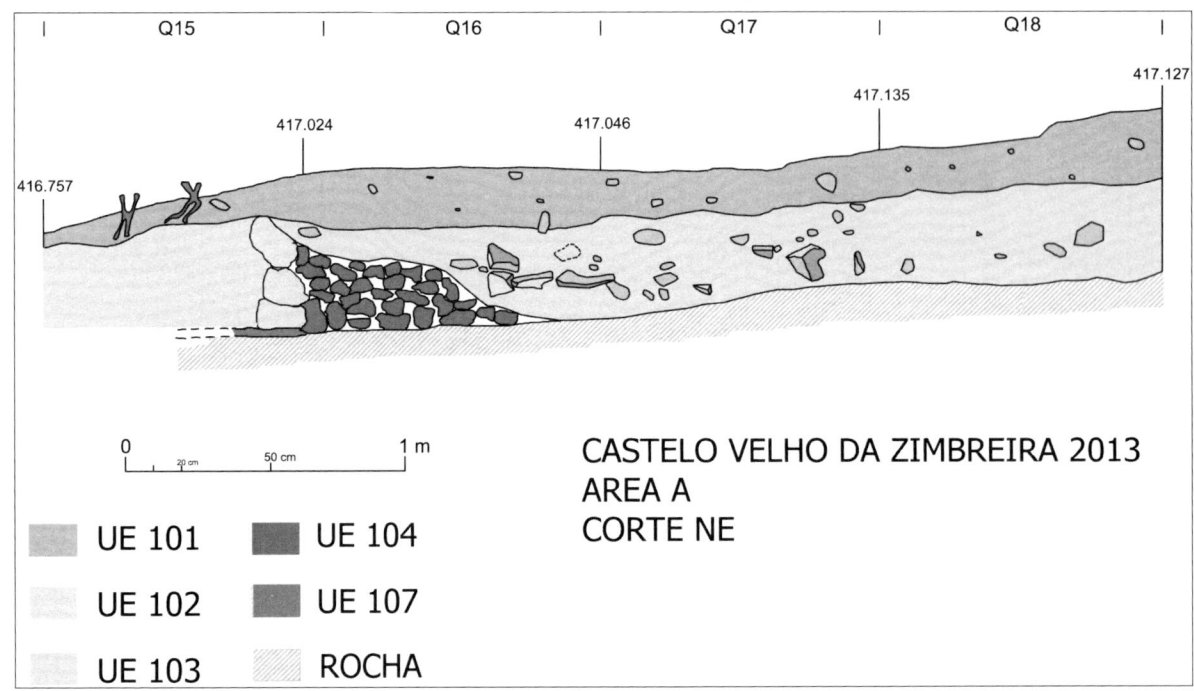

FIGURE 3. STRATIGRAPHIC SECTION OF THE INTERIOR OF WALL 2 (U.E.102 AND U.E. 104), WITH THE TWO SECONDARY DEPOSITS (U.E. 101 AND U.E. 102) AND THE CARBONACEOUS LAYER DATED BY AMS (U.E. 107) (DRAWING BY PEDRO CURA AND DAVIDE DELFINO).

Pereira 1970; Delfino *et al.*, 2013: 184-186), Castro do Santo and Castro de Amêndoa, probable Final Bronze Age walled stations (Delfino *et al.*, 2014: 193): all these archaeological monuments potentially represent a system designed to control the territory

3. Content for public distribution

Even though the research is still ongoing, a first set of preliminary and consistent data is available to provide a chronology and a basic historical view of the site; in other words the answers to the questions: what, when, how and why, can already be provided to the public at large.

WHAT: the Castelo Velho da Zimbreira is not a real settlement, but more exactly a walled and terraced station (possibly a fortified enclosure where peasants could find a safe-haven in case of danger) with very simple architectural structures

WHEN: the walled station was built sometime between the last decade of the VIII cent BC and the first quarter of the VII cent BC, probably within a short time span.

HOW: the structure is composed of dry stone walls, erected on rudimentary foundations created by digging into the rock, while at the same time creating a little passage area along the walls. Prior to the construction of walls, the hilltop had been cleaned of underbrush by fire.

WHY: in light of the strategic importance of the territory, with alluvial gold resources and the proximity of navigable tributaries of the Tagus river (Ocreza and Pracana rivers), and considering the contemporary arrival of Phoenician materials in the lower Tagus Valley during IX, VIII and VI centuries BC, it is likely that the local human communities needed to build fortified sites to defend their inhabitants and resources.

So what are the obstacles, peculiar to this site that must be overcome in order to capture public attention and facilitate an audience's understanding?
1. The walls of the site, the only monumental feature, are in an extreme state of disrepair while the integrity of the structures is also affected by the installation of a wind turbine on the hilltop;
2. The archaeological material found, 95% composed of ceramic, is in a high state of fragmentation;
3. The site is very difficult to access: even if the dirt road reached the hill top, the slope of the hill is very steep limiting access for certain categories of visitors;
4. The surrounding region is very sparsely populated and undeveloped, while the means of transportation connecting it to the more populated parts of the country are not ideal, especially in the case of public transport.

Fortunately, the site also presents certain advantages primarily linked to its spatial positioning and to the history of the monument:
1. Its high placement affords an exceptional panoramic view of the surrounding landscape;
2. The highlighted archaeological stratigraphy can provide a visual story of the station;
3. Some structures (walls) and found materials (decorated pottery) can be used to revitalize ancient technologies (burnished technique to decorate the ceramic), or technologies currently in the process of being lost (dry stone building techniques);
4. The hilltop stations' network placed around the quartzite belt allows observers to place and view the site in a broader historical and territorial context.

From a museological perspective several means and approaches to reach a broad public have been discussed in various works. We are referring here to the use of virtual reality applied to prehistoric sites (Collin-Lachaud, Passebois 2008) and archaeological monuments in general (Daly, Evans 2006), for the purpose of highlighting salient features that both define the monument and resonate with the non-specialized public (Rountree 2010), or of presenting particular issues related to pre and proto-historic monuments in a specific case in Corsica (Franceschini, Leconte-Tusoli 2006), (Franceschini, Leconte-Tusoli 2006).

The importance of the perception of the landscape as a prerequisite for placing the archaeological sites in a broader context is also highlighted (Thomas 2012: 173-176) as is the need for the creation of a link between the public and sites (Rodning 2010).

4. Tools used to spread contents

Briefly put, Castelo Velho da Zimbreira is a walled and terraced station which probably served as a refuge to the residents of the surrounding areas in case of danger, situated in a landscape characterized by a system of similar stations (at least 2 other) and settlements (at least 1) along a quartz ridge enclosing a territory possessing natural and strategic resources; the walled station arose in connection with the first direct contacts established with the Mediterranean world in the Tagus Valley (VIII-VII cent BC), perhaps suggesting a conflict for raw materials. It is immediately obvious the site presents two visible elements which can act as the basis for its popularization: 1) the dry stone walls, their monumentality in the ancient context and the building technique employed (the archaeological monument in the landscape); 2) the position of the archaeological monument in respect to the others walled stations (the holography the landscape and of the multiple walled stations and settlements).

Thus, the significance of the visual impact of the wall from the territory, and of the surrounding territory from settlement are two characteristics of the site, which are easily transmissible to the public and are easy to understand.

From this basis five types of activities have been pursued since 2010, aimed at four types of public segments (young and adult locals, elderly locals, tourists, graduate students). The activities undertaken are: a) Land Art, b) Trekking, Conviviality and Memories, c) Fieldwork and d) Virtual Reality.

4.1. Land Art on Castelo Velho da Zimbreira

In 2010, following an invitation from Professor Luiz Oosterbeek, the Director of Institute of Land and Memory in Macao, the second author was invited to produce a work of art for the project "Cultura 2007_2013/Landart Transformations", in order to reveal a local monument which was up until then unknown to the public. For this purpose the *castro* from MonteVelho was selected, and the artist visually highlighted the lines of the walls using rolls of white plastic (Gheorghiu 2012) that created highly visible landmarks. The positioning of the work in the landscape was made possible with the help of M. Pedro Cura (ITM Macao) and a small group of students.

The land-art functioned not only as an artwork but also as an instrument of landscape archaeology, since it allowed the visual analysis of the site in relation to other ancient settlements. Not only was part of the shape of the prehistoric site made visible, but the inter-sites visibility was also enhanced, during a separate experiment in 2013.

Due to its high degree of visibility within the landscape the land-art became part of the local popular culture; Portuguese television presented it explaining its meaning, and a web site designed for weather forecast in the Zimbreira area (http://www.meteo-europ.com/en/pt/santarem/zimbreira-pictures.html) added images of the artwork to the ones of local waterfalls and roads.

The land-art positioned on the mountain withstood the process of weathering efficiently and in 2013, within the Time Maps project (www.timemaps/net), designed to reveal "invisible" communities and sites on Europe's map (Gheorghiu, Delfino 2014), it was transferred to a different location, to highlight the archaeological digs in progress (Fig. 4). Again students helped the artist to position the work on the rocky slope of the mountain.

FIGURE 4. WORKING IN PROGRESS DURING THE PERFORMANCE OF LAND ART IN CASTELO VELHO DA ZIMBREIRA IN 2013, TO HIGHLIGHT THE IMPACT OF THE WALL IN THE ANCIENT LANDSCAPE.

This time the study of the inter-settlements' visibility was done on the surrounding dominant locales which supported ancient settlements, in order to observe the efficacy of the visual communications in daylight between the mountain settlements in the Bronze Age (Fig. 5).

FIGURE 5. PLACING THE WHITE TISSUE OF THE LAND ART UP
THE WALL OF CASTELO VELHO DA ZIMBREIRA IN 2013.

4.2. Trekking, Conviviality and Memories

Continuing its collaboration with the Time Maps project (Gheorghiu, Delfino 2014) and in the International Journey of Sites and Monuments, 18th Abril 2014, the Museum of Prehistoric Art of Mação has organized an activity open to young, adult and elderly locals that included in order: 1) an evening excursion from Zimbreira village to the Castelo Velho da Zimbreira; 2) an experiment of intervisibility between the Castelo Velho do Caratão settlement, the Castelo Velho da Zimbreira and the Castro do Santo walled stations using large fireplaces (Fig. 6); 3) The recounting of tales and stories about the territory and the site around the fireplace by the eldest people of Zimbreira village, while sharing hot wine and tea (Fig. 7). 130 people participated in the activity, including attendees from other locations (from Abrantes, Tomar and Coimbra city), M.A. students in Photography of the Polytechnic Institute of Tomar (provision of photography services), M.A. and PhD students in

FIGURE 6. THE FIREPLACES AT CASTELO VELHO DA ZIMBREIRA (LEFT), CASTELO VELHO DO CARATÃO (CENTER)
AND CASTRO DO SANTO (RIGHT). PICTURES BY FELIPE PEREIRA, NUNO QUEIROZ AND FLÁVIO NUNO JOAQUIM
(M.A. IN PHOTOGRAPHY, I.P.T.) © GEST.ART., I.T.M. AND TIMEMAPS.

FIGURE 7. GATHERING AT CASTELO VELHO DA ZIMBREIRA AROUND THE FIREPLACE, WITH ELDER PEOPLE RECOUNTING TALES. PICTURE BY NUNO QUEIROZ AND FLÁVIO NUNO JOAQUIM (M.A. IN PHOTOGRAPHY, I.P.T.) © GEST.ART., I.T.M. AND TIMEMAPS.

Archaeology of the Polytechnic Institute of Tomar/Trás-os-Montes e Alto Douro University (actively participating as part of the teams positioned at each site to cure the fireplaces), firemen and volunteers of the Civil Protection of Mação.

Seven elders recounted tales about the surrounding territory and Castelo Velho including childhood memories and offering valuable information about the appearance of the archaeological monument 50-60 years prior (ex. The wall was more complete at the time and reached a height equal to an adult's waist).

4.3. Fieldwork

Starting in 2012 the Land and Memory Institute (I.T.M.-Mação) has initiated an Archaeology Summer School (E.V.A.) with units in Prehistory, Later Prehistory and Protohistory, and Rock Art, with lectures, fieldworks, laboratories and excursions. Castelo Velho da Zimbreira was the fieldwork site for the unit focused on Later Prehistory and Protohistory (Fig. 8) and students (High school, Graduation, M.A. and PhD) have been participating in the field research for that walled station. In the 2011/2013 campaign the student participation in fieldwork has included students from the São Luis do Maranhão (Brasil) and Viseu (Portugal) high schools, M.A. program students in Prehistoric Archaeology and Rock Art of I.P.T./U.T.A.D. from Brazil, Portugal, Italy, Cameron, Costa Rica, Columbia and Spain, students of others M.A. programs in Archaeology from Italy, Slovenia and PhD level student from Brazil. This level of student participation has the added benefit of 'spreading the word" about the site within specialized circles, a non-negligible advantage of increased visibility for lesser known archaeological locations. In addition to the broad exposure of students from various locations, recurring fieldwork has another advantage: it provides a perfect background for directly involving the public through guided visits, interactions with the archaeological teams (which provides a different level of exposure to, and a broader perspective of the site), as well as the direct experience of "living" in contact with the ancient structures and materials. The experience of organizing guided tours during 2012 led to all these predicted results.

FIGURE 8. STUDENTS AT WORK DURING THE 2012 CAMPAIGN.

4.4. Virtual Reality

In order to produce o complete image of the site the decision was to reconstruct it in 3D. This operation allowed a re-evaluation of the archaeological research, as it included a series of data no longer accessible in the archaeological record. Under the coordination of the Portuguese team, the Romanian MA Architect Andrada Stancu (Erasmus student from the National University in Bucharest) produced a series of 3D reconstructions of the walls and the platform, visualizing the height of the surrounding walls and the access to the stronghold.

The 3D drawings were the basis for an animation of the site reconstruction in Virtual Reality, stimulating the archaeological imagination and allowing the public to understand the general shape of the Bronze Age defensive system, and to experience a tour of the walled enclosure.

4.5. Mobile Augmented Reality

To go further with revealing the Zimbreira walled enclosure to the general public and specialists, a mobile application was created as a modern tool for discovering and understanding archaeological information into its physical historical context. This is possible by using the Augmented Reality technology on mobile devices (smartphones or PC tablets) which employs the video camera and the geographical position to display different digital information over the live video of a real site. With this tool, users are empowered with the capability of seeing the real archaeological site augmented with 3D reconstructions, 2D images and explanatory texts. Furthermore, the visualization is interactive, i.e. updated with different perspectives according to users' movement and orientation, and also scaled with the distance. The application also allows users to take snapshots and further analyze the consolidated real and virtual image. The discovering process consists in showing the location of interest along with distance information and marked as a pinpoint on a Google map. To take advantage of the application is necessary to scan the following QR code with a mobile device and an internet or wireless connection.

FIGURE 9. THE QR CODE FOR STARTING THE MOBILE AR APPLICATION AND DISPLAY OF 3D RECONSTRUCTIONS IN THE PROXIMITY OF THE CASTELO VELHO DA ZIMBREIRA.

FIGURE 10. IMAGES OF THE RECREATED WALLED STATION CAN ALSO BE SEEN ON A MOBILE PHONE BY SCANNING THIS IMAGE WITH AURASMA SOFTWARE, IRREGARDLESS OF THE LOCATION.

5. Results and reflections

The 5 years of research and valorization of the Castelo Velho da Zimbreira, have physically brought on site a large number of people from the different target categories identified previously (Tab. 1).

Considering that the archaeological monument is not benefiting from any previous notoriety, as systematic excavations were only started in 2011 (with only an earlier and short rescue campaign taking place between 2004 and 2005 during the installation of the wind power generator), that the structures are similar to other hilltop walled station in Portugal (and thus have no "uniqueness" factor) and also that the region of Zimbreira is very isolated and not easily reachable without the use of a private car, the results achieved are substantial.

An important fact to be noted is that the activities involved in "living the archaeological monument" serve a double function:

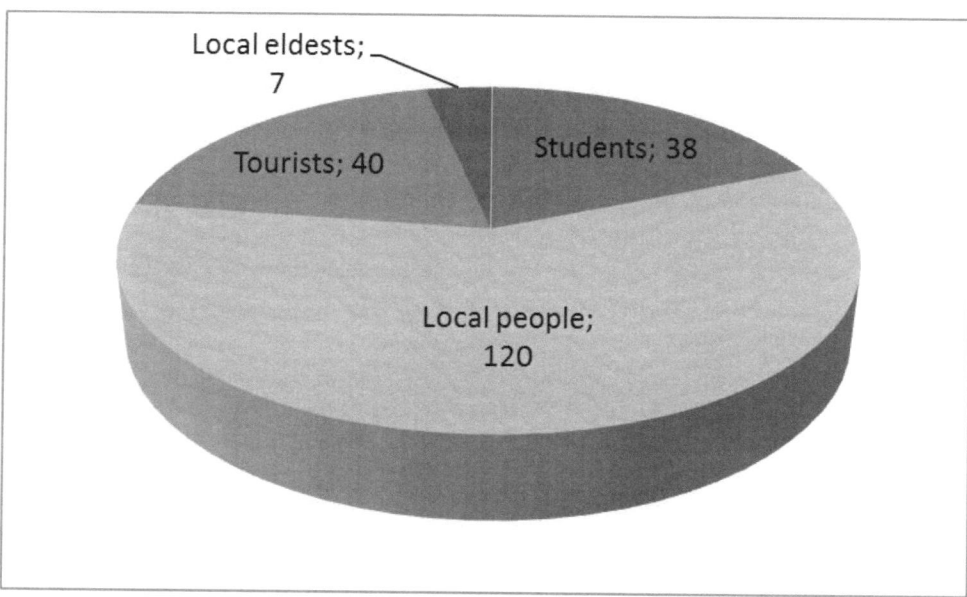

Table 1. Categories and numbers of visitors at the Castelo Velho da Zimbreira between 2010 and 2013.

1. Preservation of the site. This is achieved by raising the local inhabitants' awareness of the importance of the monument as a piece of regional heritage and by periodically "bringing life" to an almost uninhabited land and structure. Finally, preservation of the site is supported simply by the inhabitants' knowledge it exists, as the physical destruction is just the last step in a process that begins with forgetfulness of its being there;
2. Involvement of the local people, above all the elders, in an activity linked to the archaeological monuments and its related issues (landscape in transformation, ancient techniques such as dry stone building, recounting of tales, etc.). The act of "living the archaeological monument" makes the people direct participants (e.g. the elders in the act of telling stories around the fireplace), not only in the process of rescuing "living memories", but also in providing a healthy form of social help in a sparsely inhabited area where the few elderly may otherwise lead monotonous, lonely lives.

To conclude on the process of valorization of this type of archaeological monument (a prehistoric settlement/walled station), it is important to highlight the fact that in order to compensate for the lack of monumentality (compared to a megalithic burial site, a roman construction, a medieval castle, or a historical palace), one needs to emphasize the characteristics of the monument and from there build a knowledge base followed by the identification of appropriate tools for distribution of the information to the public. Obviously, the tools need to consider the prehistoric monument's potential to benefit the territory, link the monument to the landscape, talk about the monument through the landscape and talk about the landscape through of the monument. Very efficient tools that fulfill these conditions are the art performance in the prehistoric monument, and especially Land Art, as it indirectly attracts attention to the monument. The potential of simple and traditional activities should also not be underestimated, for example of stories told around the campfire. These will not be the equivalent of guided tours with an archeology lecture in the field, but they indirectly tell of the specificity of the monument. Participants living for one night as the inhabitants of the Bronze Age might have may feel afterwards interested in deeper knowledge of the monument. Finally, the use of virtual reality tools carries a great potential especially in reaching the younger generation, as well as acting as an instrument for the valorization and study of the monument.

Acknowledgements

The authors want to thank the following:
- Municipality of Mação, Parish of Envendos and Carvoeiro, Firemen and Civil Protection of Mação for the logistic and material support provided;
- Museum of Prehistoric Art of Mação, for the general support;
- MA student Andrada Stancu from the National Univeristy of Arts in Bucharest, for the 3D reconstructions;
- Professor António Martiniano Ventura and M.A. students from the Polytechnic Institute of Tomar, for the documentation support.

Last, but not least our gratitude goes to M. Bogdan Căpruciu for the proof-reading of the text.

The land art experiments in Zimbreira were possible due to two research projects (Landscape-Transformation in 2010, and *Time Maps: Real Communities – Virtual worlds – Experimented Pasts*, PN II IDEI grant in 2013).

References

ARRUDA, A. M. 2005. O primeiro milénio a.n.e. no Centro e Sul de Portugal: leituras no início de um novo século, *O Arqueólogo Português*, série IV, vol. 23, Lisboa: Museu Nacional de Arqueologia, pp. 9-156

COLLIN LACHAUD, I.; PASSEBOIS, I. 2008. Do immersive technologies add values to the museum going experiences? An exploratory study conducted at France's paleosites, *International Journal of Art Management*, vol. 11, N°. 1, Montreal: HEC, pp. 60-71.

DALY, P.; EVANS, T. L. 2006. Introduction: archaeological theory and digital past, In Daly, P.; Evans, T. L. (eds) *Digital Archaeology: Bridging Method and Theory*, New York: Routledge, pp. 3-9.

DELFINO, D. 2012. Arqueologia do contacto: dinâmicas, problemas e modelos interpretativos da Proto-História da fachada atlântica da Península Ibérica, In Oosterbeek, L.; Cerezer, J.; Bittencurt Campos, J.; Zocche, J. (eds) *Arqueologia Ibero- Americana a Arte Rupestre*, ARKEOS, 32, Tomar: C.E.I.P.H.A.R., pp. 57-70.

DELFINO, D.; OOSTERBEEK, L.; BAPTISTA, J. C.; GOMES, H.; BELTRAME, M.; CURA, P. 2013. A proto-história no Concelho de Mação: novas investigações, novas abordagens, novos dados, In Cruz, A.; Graça, A.; Oosterbeek, L.; Rosina, P. (eds) *I° Congresso de Arqueologia do Alto Ribatejo. Homenagem a José da Silva Gomes*, ARKEOS 34, Tomar: C.E.I.P.H.A.R., pp. 181-194.

GHEORGHIU, D. 2012. eARTh Vision (Art-chaeology and digital mapping), *World Art*, 2:2, pp. 211-217.

HORTA PEREIRA, M. A. 1970. *Monumentos históricos do Concelho de Mação*, Mação: Câmara Municipal de Mação.

RODNING, C. 2010. Place, Landscape, and Environment: Anthropological Archaeology in 2009, *American Anthropologists*, vol. 112, issue 2, Arlington: American Anthropological Association, pp. 180-190.

ROUNTREEE, K. 2010. Tourist attraction, cultural icons. sites of sacred encounter: Engagement with Malta's Neolithic temples, In Scott, J.; Selwyn, T. (eds) *Thinking Through Tourism*, Oxford-New York: Berg, pp. 183-208.

THOMAS, J. 2012. Archaeologies of places and landscape, In Hodder, I. (2012) *Archaeological theory today- second edition*, Cambridge: Polity Press, pp. 167-186.

VILAÇA, R.; ARRUDA, A.M. 2005. Ao longo do Tejo, do Bronze ao Ferro, *Conimbriga*, XLIII, Coimbra: Instituto de Arqueologia da Universidade de Coimbra, pp. 11-45.

E-publications

DELFINO, D.; CRUZ, A.; GRAÇA, A.; GASPAR, F.; BATISTA, A. 2014. A problemática das continuidades e das descontinuidades na Idade do Bronze do Médio Tejo português, In Cruz, A. (ed) *A*

Idade do Bronze em Portugal: os dados e os problemas, Atas da Mesa Redonda de Abrantes, *Antrope*, série monográfica 1 (2014), pp. 147-202 available in : http://www.cph.ipt.pt/download/AntropeDownload/1_2014Serie%20Monografica/ANTROPE_SM12014.pdf

GHEORGHIU, D.; DELFINO, D. 2014. Mapping invisible communities: the TimeMaps project, *O Ideário Patrimonial*, 3, Dezembro 2014, Tomar: Centro de Pré-História do I.P.T., pp. 7-26 available in: http://www.cph.ipt.pt/download/OIPDownload/n3_dezembro_2014/ideario-patrimonial-dez-2014.pdf

FRANCESCHINI, L.; LEMONTE-TUSOLI, S. 2006. The valorization of the pre- and protohistoric archaeological heritage of Corsica, from interest from practical application in the field, *Environment Identities and Mediterranean Area, 2006. ISEIMA '06. First international Symposium on*, Piscataway, NJ: IEEE, pp. 470-475, available in http://ieeexplore.ieee.org/xpl/mostRecentIssue.jsp?punumber=4150423 [accessed 15.05.2015]

Virtual palimpsests: augmented reality and the use of mobile devices to visualise the archaeological record

Dragoş GHEORGHIU
Doctoral School, National University of Arts, 19 Budişteanu Str., Bucharest, Romania

Livia ŞTEFAN
Department of Computing Applications, Institute for Computers,
Calea Floreasca 167, Bucharest, Romania

Abstract

To facilitate the archaeologists' and public's visualization of the stratigraphy of archaeological sites, we propose the use of computer-based technologies and mobile devices to achieve a palimpsest-like information layering. Specifically, we have developed a location sensitive mobile application using Augmented Reality technology and two information layers (corresponding to the Iron Age and Chalcolithic periods) on Google Maps, both providing users with a digital palimpsest of ancient habitation areas in Vădastra village (Southern Romania). The virtual layers are defined by several points-of-interest, augmented with rich archaeological and historical information, which can be individually selected and explored. The mobile application is an onsite research and educational tool, which augments the spatial and temporal perception of the past.

Keywords: *archaeological stratigraphy, virtual palimpsest, virtual archaeology, mobile devices, Augmented Reality, Google maps*

Résumé

Pour faciliter la visualisation des archéologues et du publique de la stratigraphie des sites archéologiques, nous proposons l'utilisation des technologies informatiques et des appareils mobiles pour obtenir une information superposée de la manière d'un palimpseste. Plus précisément, nous avons développé une application mobile en utilisant la technologie de la Réalité Augmentée et de deux couches d'information (correspondant à l'Âge du Fer et au Chalcolithique) sur Google Maps, les deux fournissant aux utilisateurs un palimpseste numérique des zones d'habitation anciennes dans le village Vădastra (sud de la Roumanie). Les couches virtuelles sont définies par plusieurs points d'intérêt, et sont augmenté avec de riches informations archéologiques et historiques, qui peuvent être sélectionnés individuellement et explorées. L'application mobile est un outil de recherche et d'enseignement sur place qui augmente la perception spatiale et temporelle du passé.

Mots clés: *stratigraphie archéologique, palimpseste virtuel, archéologie virtuele, appareils mobiles, Réalité Augmentée, Google Maps*

1. Introduction

In contemporary archaeology (Harris, 1989; Bentley, 2000), as in landscape studies (Balley, 2007), the site is perceived as a sequences of related layers, i.e. a palimpsest. While for archaeologists this representation is a common fact, for the public at large visual representations are necessary to facilitate this perception of the past.

In this domain the modern digital technologies play an important role in the creation of visual models that are easy to understand and manipulate. Thus, "digital reconstructions of archaeological excavation sites and their interactive visualization emerged as a powerful tool to communicate archaeological features and cultural knowledge to experts and a broad audience" (Trapp, 2012).

Information and Communication Technologies (ICT) technologies are becoming indispensable tools in contemporary archaeology research, interpretation and communication, especially in the latest decade characterized by exceptional development and diversity of capabilities and proliferation of intelligent devices (Papagiannakis *et al.*, 2008). Among the technologies that were extensively and rapidly integrated into archaeological activities we count the Geographic Information Systems (GIS), Virtual Reality (VR) and Augmented Reality (AR) as the most frequently used (Eve, 2012; Forte, 2014; Berthelot, 2015).

The mobile devices (smartphones, tablet PCs) and accessories (recent 3D visualization glasses) are becoming more technically powerful and, at the same time, affordable for the great mass of users. A whole range of free mobile applications are now available, including Google Maps, making the mobile device a sensitive and intelligent tool. For this reason mobile devices are currently the most suitable platform for AR applications.

Finally, even though there currently exist several implementations of mobile applications and AR for archaeology (Vlahakis, 2002; Papagiannakis and Magnenat-Thalmann, 2007; Magnenat-Thalmann *et al.*, 2008; Stricker, 2011; Gheorghiu and Ștefan, 2012; Gheorghiu *et al.*, 2013), they serve mostly to convey cultural heritage information to the public and less as a scientific tool.

In the present paper the authors propose the usage of mobile devices, location-aware Augmented Reality applications and free mapping systems as investigative and research tools for archaeologists, as well as educational tools for the public. The proposed solution enables accessing specialized, context sensitive archaeological information, while providing a tool for experiential learning for the public, and mainly for the younger generations, as the early adopters and main users of the enabling technology.

The paper is structured as follows: a brief survey of the state-of-the-art in computer technologies used in contemporary archaeology, a rationale of our proposal, a short presentation of the authors' previous work, a description of the solution, methods and results, and the final conclusions.

2. Computer technologies in contemporary archaeology

As already mentioned, the importance of ITC technologies in contemporary archaeology can be seen from the creation of a new sub-discipline –Virtual Archaeology (Barcelo, 2000; Nicolucci, 2002) with a new type of visualization (Bernardes *et al.*, 2012).

From this perspective, the current trend is towards perfecting the ITC tools for more realistic visualizations, a field of work which brings together archaeologist and computer specialists as "they create unique perspectives and new theoretical visions, advancing the construction of disciplinary knowledge, while making the audience extract meaning from the information being visualized" (Papadoupolos, 2010).

The research conducted on ICT technologies in archaeology spans different activities such as data acquisition and processing, documentation, modelling, interpretation, validation, visualization and communication (Forte, 2014).

Even though VR and 3D modelling are not new technologies, dating from late nineteen eighties (Hermon, 2004), they offer new virtual and smart environments both for the researcher communities and for the public spaces. Virtual Archaeology (Barceló, 2000; Niccolucci, 2002) or Cyber-Archaeology (Forte, 2014) have become a "daily tool in the investigation of human past activity and its context" (Hermon, 2004), "by visually expressing alpha-numeric data and graphically expressing thoughts and ideas" (Hermon, 2004), but mainly by facilitating the representation and understanding of abstract concepts or aspects otherwise difficult to perceive.

In the present "cyber-era" (Forte, 2014) virtual representations such as virtual museums or 3D virtual worlds, have *"the informational capacities to generate new knowledge"* (Forte, 2014) and the digitized cultural heritage enables people to experience an immersive exploration (Heim, 1997).

One method that provides access to immersion is **Augmented Reality** (AR), a computer technology related to a more general "computer-mediated reality" class of technologies (Milgram and Kishino, 1994). The reality can be augmented or diminished with computer-created (i.e. virtual) objects and information which act on the user's visual or aural perception. Specific to AR is that the virtual information is strongly related to real life information (Azuma, 1997), is generally captured by a video camera, and the merged image is projected on a head-up-display (e.g. Google glass or Microsoft Holo Lens), on a computer monitor, or on a mobile device live camera feed.

The quality of the new merged reality also gives a measure of the "presence" and immersion feeling (concepts discussed in Heeter (1992), Wagner et al. (2009), Witmer & Singer (1998), Zahorik & Jenison (1998), Pujol and Champion (2011). According to Eve (2012), the "presence means the perceptual illusion of non-mediation, and the 'user' acting in a mediated environment as if the mediation is not there".

Also in Eve (2012) it is underlined that AR in archaeology "provide(s) a timely way to combine the strengths of a computer-based approach (reproducibility, experimentation, computer reconstruction) with archaeological phenomenology (embodied experience in the field)". Archaeologists can take advantage of the AR applications to visualize and analyze different information in their real context and on a just-in-time basis (Trapp, 2012; Papagiannakis, 2010). For the public, AR is a recognized educational technology, "relevant for learning and creative inquiry" (Horizon Report, 2012) while mobile-learning is considered one of the key educational technologies for European Schools (Horizon Report, 2014).

The modern ICT technologies also allow the simulated revival of ancient places by means of character reconstructions and animations in virtual reality simulated environments: revival of life in ancient Pompeii, with virtual characters simulated in real-time using Augmented Reality (Papagiannakis and Magnenat-Thalmann, 2007) or story-based interactive storytelling (Hermon, 2004); re-enactments (Gheorghiu and Ștefan, 2012; Gheorghiu et al., 2013) or mobile AR games (Maiorescu and Sabou, 2013).

Finally, a visualization in space and time (4-dimension) for different time periods was developed for the reconstruction of the city of Koblenz (Laycock et al., 2008) by means of a "4D navigable movie" (Trapp, 2012).

Another type of computer technology frequently employed by archaeologists is **Geographic Information Systems** (GIS) which are digital interactive mapping systems, comprising both hardware and software tools. In Politis (2008) they are defined as "system(s) for capturing, storing, analyzing and managing data and associated attributes which are spatially referenced to the earth."

Using GIS in archaeology it is possible to "link information to location data, such as time to archaeological places, different earth surface levels to excavation periods, or different border lines within eras" (Politis, 2008). A great advantage of using GIS in archaeology is that it allows the use of "nonvisual data into a visual image by mapping its values into visual characteristics" (Hermon, 2006).

A broadly used GIS with applications in archaeology is **Google Maps** (GM), a public web-based GIS, which requires only a web browser and internet connection for its utilization. GM is also available on mobile devices with an offline capability – as the maps can be loaded online, and used afterward without an internet connection (offline).

GM offers the possibility to create custom layers, either by programming with Google API (application programming interface) or by means of a point-of-interest (POIs) editor. The editor allows the labeling of the POIs, as well as the attachment to them of symbols and images stored on public websites (e.g. Panoramio, Flickr). The most recent version of the GM engine expands the range of augmented information to include video recordings. The layers, comprising several POIs, can be saved and imported on other devices using a recognized file format (KML/KMZ), or can be made publically visible.

Possible examples of GIS applications in archaeology could be: Google-Earth-based meta-interface providing access to cultural data (Coralini *et al.*, 2012), or a 4-dimensional map using GM and Augmented Reality (Gheorghiu, 2012; Gheorghiu and Ștefan, 2013b).

Currently **mobile devices** offer different technical capabilities integrated into a single apparatus: photo camera, front and rear video camera, GPS receiver, sensors (gyroscope and compass), internet and wireless connectivity. The increasing processing power enables the present mobile devices to support sophisticated applications (e.g. games). The internet and wireless connections, including to social networks that can be linked to different applications, increase the ubiquity of the information.

The development of the AR technology was also conditioned by the rapid growth of the mobile capabilities (Papagiannakis *et al.*, 2008). The sensors perform the image recognition, the user's location or direction of movement, determining a precise correlation and interactivity of the displayed information.

For archaeologists, the mobile devices put them in "an authentic context and culture" (Politis, 2008), to cite only Gheorghiu and Ștefan (2012).

3. Previous work

The already mentioned potential of the ITC technologies and mobile devices was explored by the authors in different educational projects trying to transmit the archaeological information in situ at rural schools from Southern Romania (Gheorghiu *et al.*, 2013; Ștefan and Gheorghiu, 2013; Gheorghiu and Ștefan, 2014b). The acquired archaeological data from archaeological experiments was transferred as story-based re-enactments with the purpose of preserving the collection of material and immaterial heritage (Gheorghiu *et al.*, 2013; Gheorghiu and Ștefan, 2012) and afterwards was made accessible from mobile devices. Educational experimentations conducted over three years with these IT&C tools and applications showed that children quickly acquired and displayed an extraordinary ability to manipulate these instruments, and also their important educational impact, especially the AR application.

4. Augmentation as palimpsest

Following our objective to present in a clear, pedagogical manner the archaeological sites under the form of a stratigraphy – palimpsest, we used the AR potential to enable the layering of different information – textual, visual, audio and 3D objects, and also to permit a manipulation of the visualization on the screen, which further allows the implementation of a story-based scenario, while the GM layer helps to create a spatial representation.

The entire AR application is similar to an information channel, with the information contextually delivered.

The virtual information is displayed when certain conditions are fulfilled, in this case, in the proximity of geographical locations-of-interest (LOIs). Locations, and not geographical points, were defined, because the GPS precision is average and also because we wished to differentiate them from Google Maps POIs (GM POIs).

The augmentation and layering of information is complementary to the creation of a custom Google Map layer in which we attached textual and multimedia information to several GM POIs.

Both solutions, the mobile AR application and the customized and augmented GM layers could function as a **virtual interactive archaeological palimpsest**.

We were interested in visualizing the prehistoric settlements under the form of tell in the Lower Danube area which often were overlapped by Bronze Age and Roman settlements, to create archaeological multilayered sites. In our case it is a superposition of two layers of habitation, consisting of a Chalcolithic settlement (5th millennia BC) situated near the Danube (i.e. eponymous site Vădastra), which was superimposed by a Roman settlement from the second century AD.

Vădastra is an important archeological site on the map of Romania, the first prehistoric settlement dug in the 19th century (Bolliac 1872; Bolliac 1876), and which has been studied for several decades in the 20th century (Mateescu, 1974). In the last decade a number of archaeological experiments were conducted at this site (Gheorghiu, 2001; http://timemaps.net/timemap/?page_id=2533) involving the local community (Gheorghiu and Ștefan, 2012; Gheorghiu and Ștefan, 2013), with the intention of retransmitting the information on the ancient technologies to the community and an explicit historical presentation of the place.

We wanted to provide both the specialists and local community with a more explicit and easy to remember image of the Vădastra settlement, both in terms of archaeological and anthropological information. For this we defined each layer of occupation by a network of roads and points of interest, in a diagrammatic form of lines and dots.

Then we visualized the Vădastra settlement as two superimposed planes, the Roman layer overlapped over the Chalcolithic (Figs. 1, 2). These two complementary representations of the site proved their educational value, as will be shown below.

FIGURE 1. THE PREHISTORIC ROAD. VĂDASTRA VILLAGE, ROMANIA.
PHOTO AND © DRAGOȘ GHEORGHIU, 2015.

FIGURE 2. THE ROMAN ROAD. VĂDASTRA VILLAGE, ROMANIA.
PHOTO AND © DRAGOŞ GHEORGHIU, 2015.

5. Methods

In the first application we wanted to present the Roman road that connected a *villa rustica* which overlapped a part of the upper level of the Chalcolithic tell and continued along the local river valley.

A second application was designed to simultaneously present the collecting layers of dwelling of the Vădastra site dating from the Neolithic to the Iron Age. To achieve this synoptic picture of the different layers of habitat, the palimpsest model was used, i.e. overlapped layers which can be viewed together to understand the superimposed process of dwelling, in time, in a single place.

To approach the local stratigraphy the following methods were employed:

1. **The delimitation of the study area using geo-tracking methods**. The authors used an Android application ("My Tracks") which recorded under the form of a continuous track the geographic locations as they walked marking the areas where archaeological vestiges were discovered. These tracks were exported and loaded automatically as geographic layers on Google Maps using a synchronization between the mobile device and the online Google Maps server.

2. **The presentation of the augmented information in a fractal manner** (Gheorghiu and Ştefan, 2014) **presenting the stratigraphy as axonometric overlapped planes** (Fig. 3). Along the tracks we marked two locations corresponding to the centre of the delimited areas, and several LOIs defined by rigorous measurements of the geographic positions (latitude, longitude coordinates) of the archaeological finds. With the GM we defined corresponding GM POIs augmented with a) textual information; b) 2D images; c) video films with re-enactments of traditional technologies, interpreted by artists and technicians from NUA; d) assignment of chronological values to each artifact.

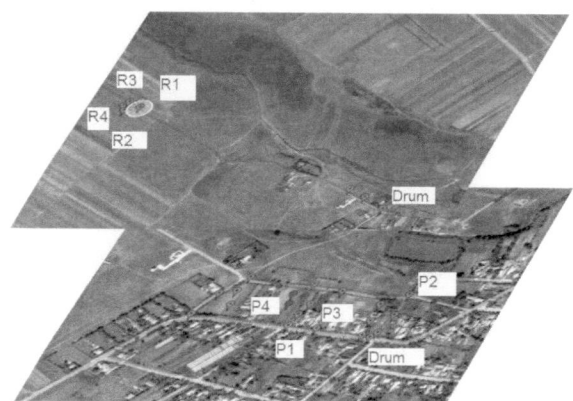

FIGURE 3. THE VIRTUAL PALIMPSEST USING GOOGLE MAPS CUSTOM LAYERS. © DRAGOŞ GHEORGHIU, 2015.

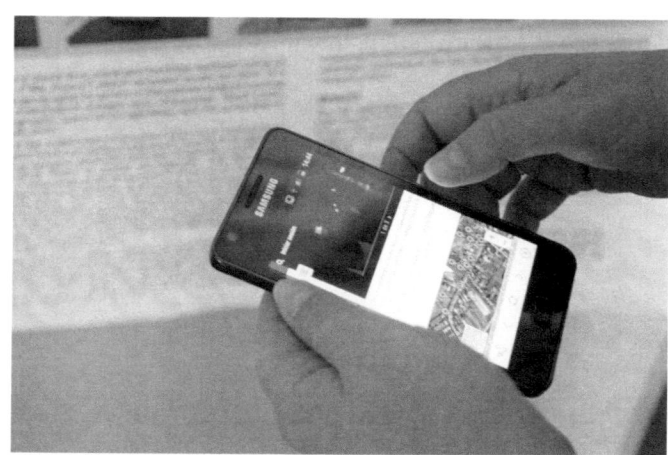

FIGURE 4. CAPTURE FROM THE "AR-PALIMPSEST" AR MOBILE APPLICATION. © DRAGOŞ GHEORGHIU AND LIVIA ŞTEFAN, 2015.

For the AR application, some LOIs were augmented with 3D reconstruction of artifacts (Fig. 4). The AR palimpsest worked as follows: when the area is geographically identified, the settlement's layers were displayed under the form of overlaid images. This palimpsest presents the archaeological stratigraphy using the axonometric planes of the most significant levels of dwelling.

When the user selects one of these planes, the architectural reconstructions of the ancient dwellings in 3D or 2D are displayed. As the user is walking and exploring the area around, several LOIs, at different fractal levels of information, are revealed (made visible), consisting in the images of the most specific objects from each architectural reconstruction, and also as video films with re-enactments.

Each LOI also displays the distance from the user's location. The dimension of the images or 3D objects is directly proportional with the distance between the viewer and them: the closer the user is to that POI, the larger the image on the screen appears.

The augmentations are described in an XML structure, which uses tags to represent different levels of information. The XML file can be modified without the need to re-install the application.

6. Results

The mobile AR application named "**AR-palimpsest**" was implemented as a Junaio AR channel (Junaio, 2015) and can be accessed by searching the name of the application in a Junaio AR client ("AR browser") that can be freely downloaded from the Android PlayStore or iOS Store. The application functions on any smartphone and Tablet PC with Android or iOS, provided that an auto-focus rear camera is available. The application can also be automatically launched by scanning of a QR barcode with the smartphones, which codifies the address of the application, similar to a web link.

On GM two layers were created, "Vădastra eponymous Chalcolithic settlement" (Google Map prehistoric layer, 2015) and "Roman road in Vădastra village" (Google Map Roman layer, 2015) tracing the approximate habitation area and marked with LOIs augmented with rich textual information, images and videos with re-enactments of traditional technologies (Figs. 5, 6). The layers are made publicly accessible; the link to the map is provided as a tiny URL name (Google Map prehistoric layer, 2015; Google Map Roman layer, 2015).

Users which only seek to discover and understand archaeological palimpsests in the area of the Vădastra village, without being able to be onsite, can explore the augmented layers on Google Maps.

Those which have a mobile device and the "**AR-palimpsest**" application will have a more complex instrument for exploration, leveraging both the augmented layers on the Google maps and the AR views.

FIGURE 5. AN AUGMENTED GOOGLE MAPS POI (THE PREHISTORIC LAYER).
© DRAGOŞ GHEORGHIU AND LIVIA ŞTEFAN, 2015.

FIGURE 6. AN AUGMENTED GOOGLE MAPS POI (THE ROMAN LAYER).
© DRAGOȘ GHEORGHIU AND LIVIA ȘTEFAN, 2015.

For a user in the proximity of the studied area, the AR application displays the two axonometric planes suggesting the main archaeological stratigraphy identified in the area of Vădastra. While the user is moving and approaching the areas of interest, more details are displayed under the form of LOIs, marked in different colors, corresponding to each archaeological layer. Each LOI (Fig. 7) can be selected and displays more information as texts, multimedia and a link to the corresponding GM layer, suggesting the chronological order and permitting the immersion in the specific architectural reconstructions to take place, in a navigation starting from general to more detailed information.

At the Vădastra site the stratigraphic palimpsest is presented under the form of two specific layers of dwelling: Chalcolithic and Iron Age. To highlight these layers, we recreated them in virtual (1) and real-virtual (2) environments, as follows: 1) by using GIS technologies, several tracks were generated to delimit the areas with archaeological interest, on which the most important LOIs were further augmented with explanatory images and video films. The user can discover these tracks using Google Maps, either on PCs or mobile devices; 2) by developing an AR application for mobile devices, which offers a high degree of interactivity: the application displays in its real context images representing the overlaid settlement layers, positioned thus to suggest a chronological order, from the most recent to the oldest layer of dwelling. By selecting an archaeological layer from the palimpsest, the application offers new levels of information on the architecture and artifacts.

The AR technology on mobile devices offered us several technological affordances. The augmentations are positioned on the screen in relation with the information received from the device's sensors and by manipulating the graphical information. For this purpose: a) the information becomes context sensitive; b) for each LOI a distance and also a direction is calculated and displayed; c) the

FIGURE 7. A LOI IN THE AR-PALIMPSEST APPLICATION.
PHOTO AND © DRAGOȘ GHEORGHIU AND LIVIA ȘTEFAN, 2015.

chronological order of information is suggested by a display in a *vertical plane* and also by different colors for the LOIs; d) the ordered display of information sequences from general to detailed, in a *horizontal plane*, was suggested by corresponding calculation of the geographical positions of the LOIs from the center of the area; e) the integration with the mapping technologies (Google Maps on PCs or mobile devices) offers a dual view; f) integration with other services, like email or social networks; g) the possibility to take and send a snapshot of the mixed reality.

7. Discussion

The AR technology on mobile devices offered us several technological affordances to create a virtual interactive and immersive archaeological palimpsest with the following advantages: a) the presentation of the information in its real context; b) the display of information in a simulated chronological order in a vertical plane and with visual clues (colors and symbols) by association with 2 LOIs situated in the center of each archaeological layer; c) the display of information in sequences from general to detailed, in a horizontal plane, by association with several LOIs disposed at a certain distance; d) the augmentation with texts, images, videos and 3D objects; e) the integration with a GIS-based mapping system, i.e. Google Maps, the mobile version.

Complementarily to these advantages, a Google Maps custom layer was created, with continuous tracks of the archaeological areas, and relevant POIs augmented with textual information, images and video films. Our solution was tested by a group of children/students, aged 8-14 years from Vădastra Secondary School during several summer campaigns. Two expeditions for discovering/ identification of the two interest zones were organized. As the children did not know these zones, they were guided only by our application "**AR-palimpsest**" which was employed as a navigation and orientation tool. The visualizations on the Google map help them identify the area and orientate towards it. Afterwards a knowledge verification was made and the children/students could visualize and place in context the archaeological data presented during the tests.

After the evaluation of the educational results of these educational experiments with children, we consider that the proposed application will prove useful in helping young people to visualize a site in context, as a palimpsest.

Another evaluation was performed during the session "Session B55 – Advances in Archaeological Palimpsest Dissection", at the XVIIth World UISPP Congress in Burgos in September 2014 (Fig. 8).

FIGURE 8. DEMO OF THE MOBILE VIRTUAL PALIMPSEST AT THE XVIIth WORLD UISPP CONGRESS BURGOS SEPTEMBER 2014. PHOTO AND © DRAGOȘ GHEORGHIU AND LIVIA ȘTEFAN, 2015.

FIGURE 9. INTERACTIVE MAP AT THE XVII WORLD UISPP 2014 CONGRESS BURGOS SEPTEMBER 2014. PHOTO AND © DRAGOȘ GHEORGHIU AND LIVIA ȘTEFAN, 2015.

The application was demonstrated interactively with a poster presentation (Fig. 9). To be able to simulate the location-awareness, in the XML file the geographical coordinates of Vădastra were modified with those of a proximity area around the University of Burgos.

The archaeologists who used their smartphones could visualize the palimpsest of Vădastra and take an immersive tour of the two dwelling levels.

As a conclusion after these, and other evaluations performed in the last three years with the Portuguese collaborators in the Time Maps research project, the authors consider that the Augmented Reality application as a virtual palimpsest will help archaeologists, researchers and other interested users, access and visualize the archaeological information in an intuitive and holistic manner.

We also consider that the AR application, a location-aware channel of information, will be useful for archaeologists, researchers and other interested users, to discover various historical sites, as well as access and visualize the archaeological information in an intuitive and integral manner.

Acknowledgements

The authors thank Mrs. Carolina Mallol and Cristo M. Hernández, organizers of the "Advances in Archaeological Palimpsest Dissection" session at XVIIth World UISPP Congress 2014, for their kind invitation to contribute to this session, and to Professor Luiz Oosterbeek and Drs. Davide Delfino and Maurizio Quagliuolo for the publishing of the present paper.

We also express our gratitude to Mrs. Laura Voicu, the Principal of the Vădastra Secondary School and to the young local community for their involvement in our experiments. Not the least, we thank Mr. Bogdan Căpruciu for kindly proof-reading this paper.

The research experiments, including the ITC, were part of the Time Maps project, a PN II IDEI grant.

Bibliography

AZUMA, R. 1997. A Survey of Augmented Reality, Presence :Teleoperators and Virtual Environments 6:4, 3-3.

BALLEY, G. 2007. Time perspectives, palimpsests and the archaeology of time, Journal of Anthropological Archaeology 26: 198-223.

BENTLEY, D. 2000. Drawings ancient and modern: phase plans and other graphics, pp. 249-256. In Roskams, S., (ed.), Interpreting stratigraphy. Site evaluation, recording procedures and stratigraphic analysis, BAR International Series 910, Oxford, Archaeopress.

BERNARDES, P.; MADEIRA, J.; MARTINS, M.; MEIRELES, J. 2012. The use of traditional and computer-based Visualization in Archaeology: a user survey, The 13th International Symposium on Virtual Reality, Archaeology and Cultural Heritage VAST 2012.

BARCELÓ, J. A.; FORTE, M.; SANDERS, D. H. (eds.). 2000. Virtual Reality in Archaeology, B.A.R. International Series 843, Oxford: Archaeopress.

BERTHELOT, M.; NONY, N.; GUGI, L.; BISHOP, A.; DE LUCA, L. 2015. The Avignon bridge: a 3D reconstruction project integrating archaeological, historical and gemorphological issues. The International Archives of the Photogrammetry, Remote Sensing and Spatial Information Sciences, Volume XL-5/W4.

BOLLIAC, C. 1872. Ceramica, Trompeta Carpatilor, XII, no. 965, p. 2.

BOLLIAC, C. 1876. Ceramica, Trompeta Carpatilor, XIV, no. 1255, p. 1.

CONOLLY, J.; LAKE, M. 2006. Geographical information systems in archaeology. Cambridge University Press.

CONROY, G. C.; ANEMONE, R. L.; REGENMORTER, J. V.; ADDISON, A. 2008. Google Earth, GIS, and the Great Divide: a new and simple method for sharing paleontological data, of Human Evolution 55(4):751-5.

CORALINI, A.; GUIDAZZOLI, A.; LIGUORI, M. C.; BAGLIVO, A.; SPIGAROLO, M. 2012. Browsing Historical Pompeian watercolours through a Google Earth-based meta interface: Luigi Bazzani's Exhibition, The 13th International Symposium on Virtual Reality, Archaeology and Cultural Heritage VAST 2012.

EVE, S. 2012. Augmenting Phenomenology: Using Augmented Reality to aid Archaeological Phenomenology in the Landscape, Journal of Archaeological Method and Theory, Volume 19, Issue 4, pp. 582-600.

FORTE, M. 2014. Virtual reality, cyberarchaeology, teleimmersive archaeology, In Remondino, F., and Campana S. (eds.), 3D Recording and Modelling in Archaeology and Cultural Heritage – Theory and best practices, BAR International Series 2598.

GHEORGHIU, D. 2001. Le projet Vădastra, Prehistorie Européenne. Université Libre de Bruxelles, Liège; p. 16-7.

GHEORGHIU, D. 2012. eARTh vision (Art-chaeology and digital mapping). World Art. 2012b; 2(2): 211-7.

GHEORGHIU, D.; ŞTEFAN, L. 2012. Mobile Technologies and the Use of Augmented Reality for Saving the Immaterial Heritage, The 13th International Symposium on Virtual Reality, Archaeology and Cultural Heritage VAST 2012, 19-21 November 2012, Brighton, UK.

GHEORGHIU, D.; ŞTEFAN, L. 2013. Preserving monuments in the memory of local communities using Augmented Reality applications, Proceedings, World Archaeological Congress, Jordan, p. 179.

GHEORGHIU, D.; ŞTEFAN, L. 2013b. The maps of time project: a 4D virtual public archaeology, 4-8 September, EAA 19th Annual Meeting, Pilsen.

GHEORGHIU, D.; ŞTEFAN, L.; RUSU, A. 2013. E-Learning And The Process Of Studying In Virtual Contexts. In M. Ivanovic si L. Jain (eds.), Studies in Computational Intelligence, Volume 528 2014, e-Learning: Paradigms and applications. Agent – based approach, Springer, ISBN: 978-3-642-41964-5.

GHEORGHIU, D.; ŞTEFAN, L.; HASNAŞ, A. 2013. Visual performances as educational tools in mobile learning, ARTSEDU 2013, 2nd World Conference on Design, Arts And Education (DAE-2013), 9-11 May, University of Architecture and Urbanism "Ion Mincu", Bucharest.

GHEORGHIU, D.; ŞTEFAN, L. 2014. Augmenting the Archaeological Record with Art (The Time Maps Project). In V. Geroimenko (ed.), Augmented Reality Art – From an emerging Technology to a Novel Creative Medium, Springer-Verlag.

GHEORGHIU, D.; ŞTEFAN, L. 2014b. 3D online virtual museum as e-learning tool. A Mixed Reality experience. The 6th International Conference on Computer Supported Education CSEDU, Barcelona.

JISC OBSERVATORY, 2011. Augmented Reality for Smartphones. A Guide for developers and content publishers. Accessed May 2015 http://observatory.jisc.ac.uk/docs/AR_Smartphones.pdf

JUNAIO web site, 2015. www.junaio.com

GOOGLE MAP PREHISTORIC LAYER, 2015. "Vădastra eponymous Chalcolithic settlement", http://tinyurl.com/ko7ylne

GOOGLE MAP ROMAN LAYER, 2015b. "Roman road in Vădastra village", http://tinyurl.com/lnfct55

HARRIS, E. 1989. Principles of archaeological stratigraphy, London, Academic Press.

HEIM, M. 1997. Virtual Realism, 1st ed., Oxford University Press, New York, NY, USA.

HERMON, S. 2004. 3D Modelling and Virtual Reality for the Archaeological Research and Museum Communication of Cultural Heritage, pp. 57-72. In Oberländer-Târnoveanu, I. (ed.), Museum and the Internet Presenting Cultural Heritage Resources On-line, Budapest, Archaeolingua.

HERMON, S. 2006. Three Dimensional Visualization and Virtual Reality in the Research and Interpretation of Archaeological Data, Accessed May 2015 from www.researchgate.net

HORIZON REPORT HIGHER EDUCATION, 2012. http://www.nmc.org/pdf/2012-horizon-report-K12.pdf

HORIZON REPORT EUROPE: 2014 Schools Edition, 2014. https://ec.europa.eu/jrc/sites/default/files/2014-nmc-horizon-report-eu-en_online.pdf

KVETINA, P.; KONCELOVÁ, M.; BRZOBOHATÁ, H.; CUMBEROVÁ, R.; CÍDKE, J.; PAVLEC, I. 2012. Neolithic settlement in Bylany: taking a new look at old digs, Progress in Cultural Heritage Preservation – EUROMED 2012.

MAGNENAT-THALMANN, N.; PETERNIER, A.; RIGHETTI, LIM, M.; PAPAGIANNAKIS, G.; FRAGOPOULOS, T.; LAMBROPOULOU, K.; BARSOCCHI, P.; THALMANN, D. 2008. A virtual 3D mobile guide in the INTERMEDIA project, The Visual Computer, Springer-Verlag, Volume 24, Numbers 7-9, pp. 827-836, July 2008, also presented in CGI08.

MAIORESCU, I.; SABOU, G. C. 2013. Learning about heritage through augmented reality games, The 9th International Scientific Conference eLearning and software for Education, Bucharest, April 25-26, 10.12753/2066-026X-13-121.

MATEESCU, C. 1974. Contribution to the study of Neolithic dwellings in Romania. A dwelling of the second phase of the Vădastra culture. Dacia NS. 1978; XXII: 65-71.

MILGRAM, P.; KISHINO, F. 1994. A Taxonomy of Mixed Reality Visual Displays. IEICE Transactions on Information Systems, 1321-1329.

NAISMITH, L.; LONSDALE, P.; VAVOULA, G.; SHARPLES, M. 2006. Literature Review in Mobile Technologies and Learning, Accessed May 2015 from www.futurelab.org.uk/research/lit_reviews.htm

NICCOLUCCI, F. 2002. Virtual Archaeology, Proceedings of the V.A.S.T. conference in Arezzo, Italy, Oxford, BAR International Series 1075.

PAPADOUPOLOS K.; KEFALAKI, E. 2010. At the computer's edge. The value of virtual constructions to the interpretation of cultural heritage, Archeomatica no 4 Decembre.

PAPAGIANNAKIS, G.; MAGNENAT-THALMANN, N. 2007. Mobile Augmented Heritage: Enabling Human Life in Ancient Pompeii, The International Journal of Architectural Computing, Multi-Science Publishing, issue 02, volume 05, pp. 395-415.

PAPAGIANNAKIS, G.; SINGH, G.; MAGNENAT-THALMANN, N. 2008. A survey of mobile and wireless technologies for augmented reality systems", Journal of Computer Animation and Virtual Worlds, John Wiley and Sons Ltd, 19, 1, pp. 3-22.

POLITIS, D.; MARRAS, I. 2008. The Use of Virtual Museums, Simulations, and Recreations as Educational Tools, pp. 157-198. In Politis, D., (ed.), 2008, E-Learning Methodologies and Computer Applications in Archaeology, New York, Information science reference.

PUJOL, L.; CHAMPION, E. 2011. Evaluating presence in cultural heritage projects. International Journal of Heritage Studies, 18(1), pp. 83-102.

STRICKER, D., ZOELLNER, M.; BISLER, A.; LUTZ, B. 2011. Traveling in Time and Space with Virtual and Augmented Reality, Accessed May 2015 from www.academia.edu

ȘTEFAN, L.; GHEORGHIU, D. 2013. Participative Teaching For Undergraduate Students With Mobile Devices And Social Networks, Proceedings of Social Media in Academics: Research and Teaching International Conference (Smart 2013), Bacau, Editura Medimond International Proceedings, ISBN: 978-88-7587-686-9, pp. 129-138.

TRAPP, M.; SEMMO, A.; POKORSKI, R.; HERRMANN, C. D.; DÖLLNER, J.; EICHHORN, M.; HEINZELMANN, M. 2012. Colonia 3D Communication of Virtual 3D Reconstructions in Public Spaces, International Journal of Heritage in the Digital Era, volume 1, No 1., pp. 44-74.

VLAHAKIS, V.; IOANNIDIS, N.; KARIGIANNIS, J.; TSOTROS, M.; GOUNARIS, M.; STRICKER, D.; GLEUE, T.; DAEHNE, P.; ALMEIDA, L. 2002. Archeoguide: an Augmented Reality guide for archaeological sites. IEEE Computer Graphics and Applications 22(5), pp. 52-60.

WAGNER, I.; BROLL, W.; JACUCCI, G.; KUUTLI, K.; MCCALL, R.; MORRISON, A.; SCHMALSTEIG, D.; TERRIN, J. J. 2009. On the Role of Presence in Mixed Reality. Presence: Teleoperators & Virtual Environments 18(4), 249-276.

WITMER, B. G.; SINGER, M. J. 1998. Measuring Presence in Virtual Environments: A Presence Questionnaire. Presence: Teleoperators & Virtual Environments 7(3), 225-240.

WOOLFORD, K.; DUNN, S. 2013. Experimental Archaeology and Games: Challenges of Inhabiting Virtual Heritage, ACM Journal on Computing and Cultural Heritage, Vol. 6, No. 4, Article 16, Publication date: November 2013.

ZAHORIK, P.; JENISON, R. L. 1998. Presence as Being-in-the-World. Presence: Teleoperators & Virtual Environments 7(1), 78-89.

TIME MAPS PROJECT. www.timemaps.net

Conservation, Preservation and Site Management at the Neanderthal Sites at Veldwezelt-*Hezerwater*, Belgium

Patrick M. M. A. BRINGMANS
The 'Veldwezelt-*Hezerwater*' Neanderthal Research Centre,
2de Carabinierslaan 18, 3620 Veldwezelt, Belgium

Abstract

The Hezerwater valley, in the brickyard quarry at Veldwezelt-Hezerwater (Lanaken, Province of Limburg, Belgium), has been an advantageous location for Neanderthal open-air settlement throughout the Middle and Late Pleistocene. During the 1995-2003 period, several stratigraphically separated Middle Palaeolithic assemblages were excavated by the Laboratory of Prehistory (Catholic University Leuven). Each year an 'Open-Day' with guided tours was organized for the general public. In total, more than 10,000 people paid a visit to the Veldwezelt-Hezerwater excavations. The massive response of the general public started the process of making the archaeological sites accessible on a permanent basis, which resulted in the 'Veldwezelt-Hezerwater Heritage Project'.

Keywords: *Veldwezelt-Hezerwater; Middle Palaeolithic; Neanderthals; Heritage*

Résumé

La vallée de Hezerwater, dans la carrière de la briqueterie à Veldwezelt-Hezerwater (Lanaken, Province du Limbourg, Belgique), avait été un endroit avantageux pour des campements de plein air néandertaliens durant le Pléistocène moyen et supérieur. Les recherches menées sur le site au cours de la période 1995-2003 ont permis le Laboratoire de Préhistoire (Université Catholique de Leuven) d'individualiser plusieurs niveaux contenant des assemblages lithiques du Paléolithique moyen au sein d'un enregistrement stratigraphique en milieu loessique. Chaque année une "Journée Portes Ouvertes" a été organisé avec des visites guidés pour le grand public. Au total, plus de 10.000 personnes ont effectué une visite. La réponse massive de la population a entraîné le "Projet Patrimoine de Veldwezelt-Hezerwater".

Mots clés: *Veldwezelt-Hezerwater; Paléolithique moyen; Néandertaliens; Patrimoine*

Introduction

The stretch of land on the left bank of the now dry Hezerwater valley in the Vandersanden brickyard quarry at Veldwezelt-*Hezerwater* (Lanaken, Province of Limburg, Belgium) has been an advantageous location for Neanderthal settlement throughout the late Middle and Late Pleistocene (Bringmans 2006). For several years, the Vandersanden company exploited the loamy fill of the asymmetrical Hezerwater valley. The industrial exploitation of the loam quarry started in 1995 and came to an end in 2003. In order to deal with the expected archaeological finds in a structured way, the 'Veldwezelt-*Hezerwater* Middle Palaeolithic Project' was started by Prof. Dr. Pierre M. Vermeersch who was the director of the Laboratory of Prehistory (Catholic University Leuven). The main field director would become Dr. Patrick Bringmans of the Laboratory of Prehistory. During the 1995-2003 period, several geological profiles were surveyed and drawn over hundreds of metres. The archaeological part of the project tried to discover and excavate Palaeolithic artefacts in the loamy matrix. The six successive summer excavation campaigns (1998-2003) provided remains of several stratigraphically separated Neanderthal sites. Except for the presence of pieces of charcoal (N=835) and animal bones (N=613), the Middle Palaeolithic finds at Veldwezelt-*Hezerwater* were exclusively lithic artefacts (N=2,500). Many scientific excursions were organized to the Veldwezelt-*Hezerwater* sites and each year an 'Open-Day' was organized for the general public near the end of the archaeological dig. In total, more than 10,000 people have paid a visit to the excavations. The massive response of the general public started the process of making the archaeological sites accessible to the general public permanently, which resulted in the 'Veldwezelt-*Hezerwater* Heritage Project'.

1. Stratigraphic Context

The most characteristic feature of the Quaternary deposits, which were studied at the Vandersanden quarry at Veldwezelt-*Hezerwater* (Bringmans 2006), is the recurrent alternation of sedimentation, weathering and denudation processes, which were called forth by climatic fluctuations (*sensu* Kukla 1977; Kukla *et. al.* 2002). Loess, loess-derived sediments and soils are usually very susceptible to these climatic fluctuations (Dansgaard *et. al.*, 1993; Van Andel and Davies 2003). In favourable conditions, as is the case at Veldwezelt-*Hezerwater*, they provide the possibility for several cycles to be studied in direct superposition. At Veldwezelt-*Hezerwater*, the late Middle Pleistocene and Late Pleistocene loess-soil sequence is strongly developed and provides detailed chronostratigraphic, palaeoclimatic and palaeoenvironmental information. The Veldwezelt-*Hezerwater* loess-soil records are now considered one of the best continental analogues of the deep-sea oxygen isotope record (Bringmans 2006). The Late Pleistocene sequence starts with a complex of soils, which has been labelled the 'Basal Soilcomplex' (Bringmans 2006). In a depression, which was created by a so-called 'spring-amphitheatre' (Gullentops and Meijs 2002), the Last Interglacial 'Basal Soilcomplex' starts with the formation of a sequence of soils (SRB-VLL-VLB). The most striking horizon of the

FIGURE 1. LOCATION OF THE NEANDERTHAL SITES AT VELDWEZELT-*HEZERWATER* (BELGIUM) IN THE VALLEY OF THE RIVER *MAAS/MEUSE*, JUST ON THE BORDER WITH MAASTRICHT (THE NETHERLANDS).

'Basal Soilcomplex' is a luvisol (PGB). Then follow two other luvisols (RB & VBLB), which were each capped by a bleached and a humic horizon. The luvisol sequence, which has been identified as the so-called 'Rocourt Soilcomplex' (Gullentops 1954), is covered by a series of distinct humic soils, which have been labelled the 'Warneton Soilcomplex' (Paepe 1967). The Last Interglacial 'Basal Soilcomplex' at Veldwezelt-*Hezerwater*, is overlain by relatively thick and differentiated Last Glacial loess/loam layers, which were further characterised by periods of interstadial pedogenesis (*e.g.*, TL, WFL & MLMB soils).

2. Archaeological Context

At Veldwezelt-*Hezerwater* (Bringmans 2006), seven *in situ* sites provided enough evidence to support the hypothesis that Neanderthals were present at there at different times during the late Middle and Late Pleistocene (Bringmans 2006; Bringmans *et. al.*, 2014b). The so-called VLL and VLB Sites (*ca.* 133,000 years BP) were characterised by laminar products (blades) and small tools, the VBLB Site (*ca.* 85,000 years BP) was characterised by medium-sized Levallois flakes and a few bifacial tools and the TL-R, TL-GF, TL-W Sites (*ca.* 58,000 years BP) and the WFL Site (*ca.* 50,000 years BP) were all characterised by big Levallois flakes and a few big Quina Tools. We think that climate and lithic raw material availability had a clear impact on the lithic variability observed within the different assemblages. The mammalian fauna from the WFL Site (Bringmans 2006; Bringmans *et. al.* 2014a) has been identified as mammoth (MNI=1), woolly rhinoceros (MNI=2), horse (MNI=5), European ass (MNI=1), steppe bison (MNI=2), reindeer (MNI=1), arctic fox (MNI=1), cave lion (MNI=1), cave hyaena (MNI=2), badger (MNI=1) and hare (MNI=1). Overall, the character of the WFL-fauna shows the existence of continental conditions. This would result in the dominance of rich open grasslands (*i.e.* the 'Mammoth Steppe' of Guthrie 1984 and 1990). The WFL faunal assemblage seems to be an example of a so-called 'horse-dominated' faunal assemblage, which could be an indication for its anthropic origin. We could thus put forward the hypothesis (Bringmans 2006; Bringmans 2014) that Neanderthals could react instrumental in creating their own life-sustaining technologies and this through interactions with the reigning environment and contacts with other Middle Palaeolithic groups.

3. The 'Veldwezelt-*Hezerwater* Heritage Project'

In the case of the 'Veldwezelt-*Hezerwater* Heritage Project', the concept of 'Public Archaeology' seemed to be very useful. The term 'Public Archaeology' was first coined by Charles McGimsey in 1972 when he published his book 'Public Archaeology' in which he discussed the past and the public access to that past, in relation to cultural resource management. Participants in this discipline would include archaeologists, architects, engineers, planners, government officials and members of public agencies. In his book McGimsey (1972) outlines his perception of what a state program in Archaeology should do and how it could set about to do it. In the case of Veldwezelt-*Hezerwater*, it turned out that the government would be the most important force behind the heritage project. The most important milestones were (1) the opening of the 'Neanderthal-Road' at Veldwezelt-*Hezerwater* on September 10, 2006, (2) the fact that site became an official listed archaeological monument on December 07, 2007, (3) the presentation of the heritage plan for the site in 2009, (4) the decision by the Flemish Government to grant a subsidy for the development of Veldwezelt-*Hezerwater* as a heritage site on August 28, 2013, (5) the start of the realization of the project in February 2014 and finally, the opening of the heritage site in June 12, 2015.

4. Why 'Public Archaeology' at Veldwezelt-*Hezerwater*?

There are at least five specific motives for presenting Archaeology to the general public at Veldwezelt-*Hezerwater*. First, the scientific community needs to generate public interest and support in order to attract funding. It is a way to publicize Archaeology and the 'excavation' process itself is most exciting to the public. Secondly, the 'Veldwezelt-*Hezerwater* Heritage Project' offers a golden opportunity to put across the point that the 'digging' process is based on careful scientific research. A third motive for practicing 'Public Archaeology' at Veldwezelt-*Hezerwater* concerned the promotion of the field of 'Neanderthal Archaeology'. Unsurprisingly, the desire to promote 'Neanderthal Archaeology' as a full-grown science stemmed primarily from the archaeologists themselves. Fourthly, the Veldwezelt-*Hezerwater* sites would also serve as a three-dimensional witness of Neanderthal presence here many thousands of years ago. And last but not least, the massive response of the general public. Each excavation season, an 'Open-Day' with guided tours was organized for the general public. In total, more than 10,000 people paid a visit to the Veldwezelt-*Hezerwater* excavations. With these five motives, the archaeologists established a sophisticated 'Public Archaeology' programme at Veldwezelt-*Hezerwater*.

Planning is the first and arguably the most important step in any heritage project (Carman and Sørensen 2009). Once the decision has been made to go beyond preserving the remainders of the Veldwezelt-*Hezerwater* sites *in situ*, the choice had to be made as to the nature and extent of the enterprise undertaken. The process of stabilizing the Veldwezelt-*Hezerwater* sites, which tried to prevent any further degradation of the archaeological monument, was of utmost importance. Planners (Carman and Sørensen 2009) should first of all remember that any disturbance of or alteration to any archaeological site compromises its integrity and destroys contextual information. So, 'proper practices' (Carman and Sørensen 2009) should minimize the impact on the Veldwezelt-*Hezerwater* sites and ensure its protection and preservation. This included first of all adequate infrastructure to support visitors. For instance, carefully planned pedestrian walkways should avoid destructive effects of increased foot traffic through the Veldwezelt-*Hezerwater* sites, avoiding leaning, climbing, sitting or standing on archaeological remains. However, the protection and the development of the Veldwezelt-*Hezerwater* sites should not result in the complete alteration of the original character of the archaeological sites.

5. The Veldwezelt-*Hezerwater* Heritage Site

5.1. The Concept

As a general rule, the visit to the Veldwezelt-*Hezerwater* sites will always take place under the guidance of an official and professional guide. However, as the process of discovery is one of the most important aspects of on-site archaeological experiences, the visitor of the Veldwezelt-*Hezerwater* sites will not get an instant overview of the whole area when he or she enters it, but will gradually discover the Neanderthal sites by following different walkways. These concrete walkways, which take visitors along pre-determined routes, allowing them to experience an environment of archaeological significance. The route has a clear start and end point, passing through a wider archaeological environment. The walkway had to provide comfortable and equitable access for all visitors, including persons with disabilities. The path itself has a continuous clear width and free height, and a smooth surface which has no major obstacles and no steep gradients. The insertion of information panels and railings was not undertaken without considering the impacts of such items on the perceptions by the visitors. The short texts on the information panels are adapted to this approach. There is little text used and here and there a word or an image is used that requires additional explanation by the guide. Given the necessity of bridging great differences in altitude the visitor gradually goes back in time. The present tour, in which a professional guide introduces the public to the practice of Archaeology within the context of excavations, is surprisingly reminiscent of the 'Public Archaeology' efforts in Veldwezelt-*Hezerwater* nearly fifteen years earlier, when the archaeologists themselves guided visitors around within the context of the ongoing excavations.

The story that is being told during the on-site tour, is that of the life of the Neanderthals. In addition to the main storyline, there are also other secondary themes, including the origin and the development of the landscape, the influence of the climate on the landscape and aspects of palaeoanthropology. The protection of the original quarry walls and surfaces, is realized by means of roof constructions,

FIGURE 2. VISITORS PARTICIPATING IN GUIDED WALKING TOURS AT THE VELDWEZELT-*HEZERWATER* SITES DURING THE 'OPEN DAY' IN 1998, WHILE THE ARCHAEOLOGISTS ARE TALKING ABOUT THEIR RECENT DISCOVERIES.

which are integrated into the surrounding landscape. The structures, which give a specific character and identity to the Veldwezelt-*Hezerwater* sites, are visible from the surrounding landscape, and take a 'landmark-function' for recreationists and visitors. The on-site tour follows a fixed route along the three main geological profiles, which have been protected by metal roof constructions. The tour starts at the entrance gate and the visitor makes a jump in time from the present to 133,000 years ago. The long walkway, which starts at the gate, brings the visitor straight to the oldest sites (*ca.* 133,000 years old). Then the visitor walks back to the entrance gate along the three main geological profiles, which contain the remainders of the other sites, respectively *ca.* 85,000, 58,000, 50,000 and 47,000 years old. The lay-out of the walkway presents the different sites in a chronological order, which allows the visitors to literally climb back to the present. In addition, there are also some 'excursions' included in the text on the information panels. These excursions serve as additional background information during the tour. Themes as 'the Middle Palaeolithic', 'the Neanderthal', 'the Pleistocene', 'Climate Change' *etc.* are being dealt with. These themes are raised at the most logical spot during the tour. How this additional information is presented to the visitor is left to the guide. During the tour, the guide can pause at the so-called 'resting spots'. Here open-air benches were installed, which enable the visitor to sit down while the guide provides him with additional information.

5.2. The Entrance Gate

The primary function of the entrance gate is to 'seal off' the archaeological sites. The sites are only accessible when being accompanied by an official guide. At the same time, the entrance gate functions from the outside as a 'trigger' for the casual passer-by. It draws the attention and at the same time it triggers the imagination. Next to the gate, there is a text panel, which briefly explains the purpose of the gate and the presence of the Veldwezelt-*Hezerwater* archaeological sites. The text panel also provides the passer-by with the contact information. So, interested people can make an appointment. The panel also shows the logos of the partners who are involved in the realization of the project. The gate itself is formed by horizontal bars. These depict the stratigraphic sequence of layers that can be seen while visiting the sites. Between the 'layers' of the gate, objects, which are typical for each time period can be found. The gate actually functions as some sort of timeline. The chosen objects refer to important inventions during human prehistory and history. These objects can also be found on the timeline, which can be seen while going down the concrete access walkway. In most cases, these images will be meaningful to the average visitor. For instance, the image of a smartphone represents today, the image of a typical Roman helmet represents the Romans, a classical Greek temple represents Classical Greece and so on. There is also an image of a Neanderthal and an Anatomically Modern Human walking side by side. Next to the entrance gate, a large boulder can be seen. It is called a 'boundary stone' and it was placed there by the '*Grensschap Albert Canal*' and functions as a landmark.

5.3. The Timeline Beyond the Entrance Gate

At the gate, the guide will introduce the archaeological site to the visitors. Then the visitors will go down the long walkway between the entrance gate and the oldest archaeological levels. This will allow the visitor to get an idea of prehistoric time. The walkway itself is a physical timeline on which the visitor walks from the present to 133,000 years ago. It is a walk from the present surface of the Earth to the surface of the Earth 133,000 years ago. At the lowest level of the walkway, the visitors will be able to stand on the same ground as the Neanderthals stood some 133,000 years ago. This deepest level is situated about 15 metres below the present surface. The purpose of this timeline is double: on the one hand one gets physical insight into deep Palaeolithic time, which distances ourselves from the Neanderthal communities who were actually living here. On the other hand, the visitor is taken back in time, as it were, to the oldest human traces, which can be found

FIGURE 3. THE MAIN GEOLOGICAL PROFILE AT VELDWEZELT-*HEZERWATER*, WHICH INCORPORATES THE REMAINDERS OF ALL THE MAJOR ARCHAEOLOGICAL HORIZONS, IS NOW PROTECTED BY THE CHARACTERISTIC ROOF CONSTRUCTIONS.

here. There are actually two timelines along the walkway. On the left side, several images refer to important events during human history and prehistory. A second series of symbols refers to the on-site presence of the Neanderthals here. The images represent stone tools that have been excavated at the Veldwezelt-*Hezerwater* sites. Each lithic tool represents one site and is placed on the exact spot on the timeline. The same tools come back later on the information panels at the different sites and on the stratigraphic levels to indicate the presence of Neanderthal sites. On the right side, one can see the images of the prehistoric animals that were living here in the valley of the Hezerwater. At the end of the walkway there is an information panel on which a map can be seen. Veldwezelt-*Hezerwater* and other important prehistoric sites in the region (Bringmans *et. al.*, 2005) are indicated.

5.4. The VLL-VLB Geological Profile Wall

The VLL-VLB Sites are the oldest sites and they were inhabited by Neanderthals around 133,000 years ago. Next to the main profile wall at the VLL-VLB Sites an information panel can be seen. On the basis of the analysis of the composition of the different layers and soils, it is possible to reconstruct the landscape and the climate. The position of the artefacts in a sequence of layers enables the archaeologist to date the archaeological sites. This gives us an idea when Neanderthals were present in the region. All this information was initially 'hidden' in the profiles, which for a layman or the average visitor will be difficult to grasp. However, the visitors themselves can observe the colour differences in the geological profile with the naked eye. The symbols of the lithic tools are shown on the information panels at the height of the actual level of the site in the profile. It is important that the guide explains the concept of an archaeological 'living floor'. This generic and imprecise term is applied to an assumed level of occupation within an archaeological site. Neanderthals were thus not living in profiles, but they were walking around on a living floor, which was the actually surface of the Earth at that time.

5.5. The VBLB Geological Profile Wall

Then the tour will bring the visitor to the second geological profile wall, which actually represents the highest point of the excavated area. Here, the VBLB Site with an age of 85,000 years was excavated. The visitors should make their own observations first, followed by the explanation of the guide. The information panel provides the same information as at the previous profile wall. The text on these panels is intentionally limited. It is not intended to include all the information given by the guide. This makes it possible to differentiate the information according to the group that is visiting the site. The text on the information panel sums up the most important information. The guide can elaborate on some elements. For instance, at the VBLB Site, the lithic artefacts were concentrated in two different zones. One zone represented a tool production area and the other zone represented an area for tool usage. It is thus possible to talk at this point about intra-site settlement dynamics. On the information panel a large evocation drawing can be seen. The general environment from 85,000 years ago is reconstructed. The river can be seen in the background. A group of Neanderthals is producing stone tools and a hearth is lit. This reconstruction is based purely on scientific observations.

5.6. The TL-WFL-MLMB Geological Profile Wall

The TL Site is about 58,000 years old, the WFL Site must be dated around 50,000 years ago and the MLMB Site is probably 47,000 years old, which makes it the youngest open-air site in Belgium and even in the Benelux. Next to the main TL-WFL-MLMB profile wall an information panel can be seen. The same information as at the two other profile walls is provided here. At the WFL Site the presence of a 'hyena den' has been observed (Bringmans 2006). The presence of this 'hyena den' complicates the interpretation of the bones excavated at the WFL Site, since there obviously could be a mixture between a Neanderthal occupation site and a carnivore habitat. Besides the problems associated with a simple taphonomic model (*i.e.*, the 'diachronic' mixing of two different human and animal habitats), more complex models are possible. The Neanderthals who were living at the MLMB Site

Figure 4. A Neanderthal and an Anatomically Modern Human walking side by side, detail of the iron entrance gate at Veldwezelt-*Hezerwater*.

at Veldwezelt-*Hezerwater* around 47,000 years ago, which is the youngest open-air site in Belgium and even in the Benelux, are just a little older than the first Anatomically Modern Humans in Eurasia, who were actually living in Siberia. Indeed, Ust'-Ishim Man (Fu *et. al.* 2014), who is dated around 45,000 years ago, was the first known Anatomically Modern Human in Eurasia. Analysis of the genome of Ust'-Ishim Man (Fu *et. al.*, 2014) revealed that his subspecies interbred with Neanderthals between 86,000 and 37,000 years ago. It has been proven that the DNA of Anatomically Modern Humans outside Africa contains between 1.5 to 2.1 percent DNA of Neanderthal origin (Fu *et. al.*, 2014). While the visitors can reflect on these scientific discoveries, they reach the entrance gate of the Veldwezelt-*Hezerwater* sites. This is where the guided tour ends.

6. The Risks and Benefits of 'Public Archaeology' at Veldwezelt-*Hezerwater*

Although Prof. Dr. Pierre M. Vermeersch and Dr. Patrick Bringmans always supported the concept of 'Public Archaeology', they were aware that not all archaeologists and palaeoanthropologists shared the same enthusiasm for this kind of approach. Indeed, some researchers believe that public outreach not only is a nuisance to archaeologists, but that there is always a real threat of vandalism. Rejecting this attitude toward the visiting public early on, Vermeersch and Bringmans started to organise 'Open-Days' with guided tours at the Veldwezelt-*Hezerwater* excavations. This approach would set the stage for the development of the 'Veldwezelt-*Hezerwater* Heritage Site' fifteen years later. The concerns over the possible destructive consequences (*e.g.*, looting and vandalism) of a public outreach like that at Veldwezelt-*Hezerwater* are however legitimate. Even McGimsey (1972) simultaneously acknowledged and tried to minimize these concerns by stating that public outreach at the end of the day would be beneficial for everyone involved. Many professional archaeologists have since tried to demonstrate the benefits of 'Public Archaeology'. For instance, Stone (1997) and Little (2002) showed that the benefits are numerous and diverse, and they concluded that any attempt to realize such benefits is well worth the risk. The successful program of 'Public Archaeology' at

Veldwezelt-*Hezerwater*, which included 'Open-Days', guided tours of the excavations and on-site exhibits, together with the massive response of the general public, shows that archaeologists have an obligation to participate in programs that attempt to explain scientifically generated archaeological information to the lay public.

7. Conclusion

The 'Veldwezelt-*Hezerwater* Middle Palaeolithic Project', which was started by the Laboratory of Prehistory (Catholic University Leuven), provided remains of several stratigraphically separated Neanderthal sites. The massive response of the general public to the archaeological excavations at Veldwezelt-*Hezerwater* started the process of making the archaeological sites accessible to the general public permanently, which resulted in the 'Veldwezelt-*Hezerwater* Heritage Project'. The final step in the process was the creation of the 'Veldwezelt-*Hezerwater* Heritage Site'. The protection of the original quarry walls and surfaces, was realized by means of roof constructions, which were integrated into the surrounding landscape. The development of the 'Veldwezelt-*Hezerwater* Heritage Site' did not result in the wholesale change of the original archaeological site and landscape, but preserved the sites as they were left behind by the excavating archaeologists. The enthusiastic and sincere efforts of Prof. Dr. Pierre M. Vermeersch and Dr. Patrick Bringmans and others to present Pleistocene Archaeology to the general public in Veldwezelt-*Hezerwater* are a direct consequence of the responsibility they genuinely felt to engage the general public in their scientific work. A large part of this sense of responsibility was a direct result of the nationally recognized importance of the Veldwezelt-*Hezerwater* Neanderthal sites they were excavating. Archaeologists have a duty to reach out to the general public, and they need to participate in projects of interpretation and outreach, with the aim of improving the conservation, preservation, protection and interpretation of archaeological heritage sites.

Acknowledgements

The "Laboratory of Prehistory" in the former "Earth Sciences Building" in the Redingenstraat (*Katholieke Universiteit Leuven*, Belgium) was an intellectual home base for me during the time that much of the work was done for this study. The "Veldwezelt-*Hezerwater* Middle Palaeolithic Project" research team was headed by Prof. Dr. Pierre M. Vermeersch. The other team members were Prof. Dr. Frans Gullentops, Prof. Dr. Jean-Marie Cordy, Ir. Jean-Pierre de Warrimont, Albert J. Groenendijk and Drs. Erik P.M. Meijs. The team members helped me to formulate some of the methods, techniques and ideas that appeared within this study. I would also like to thank Peter Ramakers and I appreciate the insightful discussions and difficult questions that we dealt with, all of which make this a better study.

Funding is gratefully acknowledged from the Institute for the Archaeological Heritage (I.A.P., Belgium) of the Flemish Community, the Provincial Gallo-Roman Museum (Tongeren, Belgium), N.V. Vandersanden Steenfabrieken (Spouwen, Belgium), the Fund for Scientific Research – Flanders (F.W.O., Belgium), the Province of Limburg (Belgium), the Province of Limburg (The Netherlands), BPF-*Bouw* (The Netherlands), the Community of Lanaken (Belgium), the Community of Riemst (Belgium) and the City of Maastricht (The Netherlands).

References

BRINGMANS, P. M. M. A. 2006. Multiple Middle Palaeolithic Occupations in a Loess-soil Sequence at Veldwezelt-Hezerwater, Limburg, Belgium. Ph.D. Dissertation. Katholieke Universiteit Leuven. 418 p.

BRINGMANS, P. M. M. A. 2014. Late Pleistocene Neanderthal Occupation in the Meuse River Basin in Belgium: Wandering Hunter-gatherers or Stocky Cave-dwellers? In Chacón, M. G.; Rivals, F. eds. lits. – Session A21a – Neanderthals on Their Own Terms: new perspectives for the study of Middle Paleolithic behavior. Atapuerca: the XVII World UISPP Congress, Union International de Sciences Préhistoriques et Protohistoriques, Burgos, 1-7 September 2014. Book of Abstracts. Burgos. p. 488.

BRINGMANS, P. M. M. A. [*et. al.*], 2005. Neanderthals at Kesselt-*Op-de-Schans*. Interim Report on the Excavation of the VBLB-Site (85 ka) at Kesselt-Op-de-Schans (Limburg, Belgium). Katholieke Universiteit Leuven. 15 p.

BRINGMANS, P. M. M. A.; DE WARRIMONT, J.-P.; CORDY, J.-M. 2014a. Neanderthals and Their Fellow Travellers on the 'Mammoth Steppe': A 'Horse-dominated' Faunal Assemblage from the 50 ky BP Middle Palaeolithic WFL-Site at Veldwezelt-*Hezerwater*, Belgium. In Fernández-Lomana, J. C. D.; Brugal, J.-P. eds. lits. – Session B35 – Paleolithic Archaeozoology: Advances on hunter-gatherer's subsistence. Atapuerca: the XVII World UISPP Congress, Union International de Sciences Préhistoriques et Protohistoriques, Burgos, 1-7 September 2014. Book of Abstracts. Burgos. p. 892.

BRINGMANS, P. M. M. A. [*et. al.*], 2014b. Neanderthal Lifeways in North-West Europe: The Challenge of the 'Eemian' Forest. In Lanata, J. L.; Lozano, S.; Martínez-Navarro, B. eds. lits. – Session A2f – Pleistocene Human Dispersals: climate, ecology and social behavior. Atapuerca: the XVII World UISPP Congress, Union International de Sciences Préhistoriques et Protohistoriques, Burgos, 1-7 September 2014. Book of Abstracts. Burgos. p. 89-90.

CARMAN, J.; SØRENSEN, M. L. S. 2009. Heritage Studies: an Outline. In Sørensen, M. L. S.; Carman, J. eds. lits. – Heritage Studies: Methods and Approaches. Milton Park, Abingdon, Oxon. p. 11-28.

DANSGAARD, W. [*et. al.*], 1993. Evidence for General Instability of Past Climate from a 250-kyr Ice-core Record. *Nature* 364: p. 218-220.

FU, Q. [*et. al.*], 2014. Genome sequence of a 45,000-year-old modern human from western Siberia. *Nature* 514: p. 445-450.

GULLENTOPS, F. 1954. Contributions à la chronologie du Pléistocène et des formes du relief en Belgique. Mémoires de l'Institut Géologique de l'Université de Louvain 18: p. 125-248.

GULLENTOPS, F.; MEIJS, E. P. M. 2002. Loess sequences in Northern Haspengouw, Belgian Limburg. In Ikinger, A.; Schirmer, W. eds. lits. – Terra Nostra. Schriften der Alfred-Wegener-Stiftung 02/1. Loess units and solcomplexes in the Niederrhein and Maas area. Joint Symposium of the DEUQUA, BELQUA and Deutsche Bodenkundliche Gesellschaft / Arbeitskreis für Paläopedologie. Neuss, 9-12 Mai 2002. Heinrich Heine University. Düsseldorf. p. 80-91.

GUTHRIE, R. D. 1984. Mosaics, allelochemics and nutrients: an ecological theory of Late Pleistocene megafaunal extinctions. In Martin, P. S.; Klein, R. G. eds. lits. – Quaternary Extinctions: a Prehistoric Revolution. Tucson, Arizona. p. 259-298.

GUTHRIE, R. D. 1990. Frozen Fauna of the Mammoth Steppe. Chicago-London. 172 p.

KUKLA, G. J. 1977. Pleistocene land-sea correlations: Europe. *Earth-Science Reviews* 13: p. 307-374.

KUKLA, G. J. [*et. al.*], 2002. Last Interglacial Climates. *Quaternary Research* 58: p. 2-13.

LITTLE, B. J. 2002. Public Benefits of Archaeology. Gainesville. 304 p.

MCGIMSEY, C. R. 1972. Public Archeology. New York. 265 p.

PAEPE, R. 1967. The Rock Sequences of the Late Pleistocene. The Stratigraphy and the Palaeobotany of the Late Pleistocene in Belgium. Geological Survey of Belgium 8: p. 1-57.

STONE, P. G. 1997. Presenting the Past: A Framework for Discussion. In Jameson, J. H. Jr. eds. lits. – Presenting Archaeology to the Public: Digging for Truths. Walnut Creek. p. 23-34.

VAN ANDEL, T. H.; DAVIES, W. 2003. Neanderthals and modern humans in the European landscape during the last glaciation: archaeological results of the Stage 3 Project. McDonald Institute Monographs. Cambridge. 265 p.

The scientific value of replicas through the analytic experience of Magdalenian portable art

Roberto ÁVILA
Muséum National d'Histoire Naturelle – Paris, France*
Universitat Rovira i Virgili – Tarragona, Spain
robertt.avila@gmail.com

Abstract

This research aimed in comprehending the scientific value of portable art replicas through examination of extrinsic and intrinsic aspects of the artifacts and, later, by comparing a sample of replicas to their matched authentic objects. Whilst some casts failed in maintaining natural features present on the genuine artefacts, relying, then, on a good documentation in order to be reliably studied, others have responded well in regard to their "decorative" aspects. By demonstrating that casts can be successfully used in scientific analysis, this paper raises insights for the study of collections and the healthy conciliation between research and conservation of objects.

Keywords: *Portable Art, Magdalenian, Replicas, Documentation, Museology*

Résumé

La recherche avait l'objectif de comprendre la valeur scientifique des moulages d'art mobilier. Les éléments de preuve extrinsèque et les caractéristiques intrinsèques des objets ont été examinés et, par la suite, un échantillon de répliques a été comparé aux objets authentiques. Alors que certains moulages ont échoué dans le maintien des caractéristiques naturelles présentes dans les objets authentiques, donc dépendent d'une bonne documentation de l'artefact original afin d'être étudié de manière fiable, d'autres ont bien répondu en ce qui concerne les aspects "décoratif". En montrant que les répliques peuvent être utilisées pour des analyses scientifiques, ce document définit de nouvelles perspectives pour l'étude des collections et le lien entre la recherche et la conservation des objets d'art mobilier.

Mots clés: *Art Mobilier, Magdalénien, Moulages, Documentation, Muséologie*

1. Introduction

The analysis of archaeological collections is a promising field for two main reasons. The first is the pressing necessity to meet countless collections conditioned (or packaged) in institutions with no studies for several decades. The second ground is the low cost of this research mode, especially for the scientific initiation of new archaeologists when funds to fieldworks are scarce. The two motifs, when summed, contribute in the preparation of material for exhibitions and publication in the academic sphere or to the general public, as well as opening up room for new considerations and starting points.

The present paper, product of the master thesis of the author (Avila 2014), sought to fit in this debate. For that, a series of portable art objects for long conditioned at the IPH[1] were selected to be descriptively analyzed. The series was set at the Magdalenian period from the region of Dordogne, France. The research had the objective to elaborate a descriptive report in order to fulfill a couple of multidisciplinary tasks through specific approaches. The production of well cataloged and systematized data is essential for a natural development of scientific research.

---

* In the moment of presentation of the poster in UISPP congress in Burgos the author was enrolled as a master student in the URV – Tarragona but he developed its master dissertation at MNHN – Paris, where his mobility period took place.
[1] Institut de Paléontologie Humaine – Paris.

As result of the analyses – following the high number of portable art reproductions on the addressed collection – it came to our attention the necessity to approach the role and the scientific import of replicas in archaeology. Indeed, the analyses of the replicated artefacts have proved really satisfactory regarding their decorative aspects, but frail as to their physical characteristics. Then, we try to understand how to complement this fragility and to give the proper scientific value to replicas for they have a bright and soothing benefit: the preservation of artefacts.

2. Replicas: scientific relevance and didactic value

Replicas, or casts, are replicated objects thoughtfully resembling the respective original artefacts concerning their overall shape and appearance, though usually made on different material. They may have historical, scientific and/or educational purposes within museums, schools, universities, institutions and research in general. Nowadays their main concern lies on the preservation of original artefacts that, in many cases, might be too frail or their display poses them in risk from diverse agents. All in all, these reproductions of artefacts help to provide a material representation of the past at the same time that preserve the original objects. Also, in contrast to an original piece that has uniquely its intrinsic value, a replica has a double value: [1°] the incarnation of the original object that was replicated and [2°] the scientific issue that materializes the reason for researchers have wished to possess a copy. They are *"witness of a particular state at a given time and do not undergo the same process of degradation as the works in situ, acquiring a memorial value even though the originals have lost representative value or have been destroyed"*[2] (Guillemard, apud Antonini 2012, p. 7). In this respect, replicas of Palaeolithic art are a kind of snapshot of the history of prehistory as a scientific discipline, besides to carry the same informational load of symbolic, social and economic aspects of the life of prehistoric men as well as authentic artefacts. In other words, to make a reflection on this peculiar subject compels us to approach questions on anthropology, sociology, history of art and science, as well as the archaeology as discipline itself.

2.1. Brief history of moulages and their fluctuations of value

Best known in France as "moulages", the replication of archaeological objects have some interesting nuances over the history of science, particularly in archaeology. But it is not easy task to tell a history of the replicas. Each country, each region and even each museum has its own histories to be told, with their own obstacles and particularities. In general sense, despite replicas have had several different roles since Roman times (Falser 2011), it is throughout the nineteenth century that casting practices will experience a growing popularization.

Many fluctuations in significance have taken place since then. These alterations eventually have transformed the functions of the replicas and the way people saw them, either in art or in science. Previously to the use of replicas, "the discovery of archeology, for instance, fell essentially within paper museums, exhibition places and construction tools for a speech" (Hurel 2010:141). In sum, primarily as an object of aesthetic attention (Barbanera 2000 [*passim*]), the moulage was gradually reduced onto a historic dimension with scientific goals, progressively becoming an object of experimentation. In the last three decades, however, collections of replicas – that for many years were considered "wreckage" of an archeology overtaken for not being in conformity with the new modern methodologies – came to be taken into consideration once again, and, thus, plenty of reflections on their history and their function in time began slowly to emerge. From the 1980s onwards, as were in the 1870s (Crocquevieille 2008), they are often used in teaching by offering an impression of scale and three-dimensional qualities that no picture can provide. Replicas were once a primary vehicle for art education, and later for science, but when the classical ideals they represent fell out of fashion, so did the replicas. Many cast collections were broken, destroyed or, at best, relegated to

---

[2] Freely translated from the original: "...témoins d'un état à un moment donné et ne subissant pas les mêmes processus de dégradation que les oeuvres in situ...", "...acquièrent une valeur mémorielle alors même que les originaux ont perdu toute valeur représentative ou sont détruits...".

basements in the course of the twentieth century, for numerous museums could no longer see utility for them. Hence, the casts became bearers of *"negative values that made them be disregarded as an object with value, not justifying, so to say, their conservation"* (Gamboni *apud* Antonini 2012, p. 5). Therefore, currently, institutions should consider themselves very lucky to have their cast collections, for replicas will become an increasingly valuable record of lost or damaged objects, as well as an impressive and intriguing reflection of the taste of the curators and the public of the late XIX century. Thus, casts have their own story to tell about the history of collecting – and about the rise and fall of prevailing tastes. In other words, currently, a cast not only represents and symbolizes the original artefact, but also conquered the historical value that renders it as an historical artefact itself, granting to a collection of casts a triple role: to speak to audiences in expositions, to be used for research and comparison, but also to be preserved as any other artefact (Antonini, 2012).

2.2. Multi value of replicas and their current applications

Nowadays replicas have two major applications: didactic and scientific. The primary purpose of moulages is educational, since institutions and museums need models in three dimensions in order to access the form, the textures, the themes, the anatomy, and aesthetical features in general, establishing then a proper practical manual of replicas. Moreover, plenty of schools and colleges of archaeological vocation choose to have their own "pedagogical valises", which regroups representative objects of a determined period, a particular society or a specific sort of activity. Aiming to be complete and manageable, samplings are composed mostly by copies. The reconstitution in museum serves, then, as element of museographic support for disclosure as well as educational tool for personal and collective formation.

Within universities, collections of casts are complementary to archeology and art history courses due to their completeness and for they allow to study the evolution of forms. In archeology institutions they are more than just an educational tool, but rather a supplement for laboratories, libraries and original collections. In these environments, a second purpose of the replicas is the scientific interest: the cast allows restoring a vanished state of the original, when the latter has been transformed by restorations, arrived in bad conditions or without its complete composition. A researcher may not always be based on the original piece which interests him, particularly when this same piece is kept abroad. He can though study the exact replica of the artefact. For this reason, a laboratory that brings together an extensive replicated collection of human remains (cranial and post cranial), for example, becomes a powerful tool for understanding human evolution. This also is employed to faunal remains, to bone and/or lithic industries, and, peculiarly, to portable art. The technique also allows making multiple specimens of the same artefacts, providing the possibility to several researchers throughout the world to work on the same objects.

But those are not the only employments; reconstitution can be regarded as a scientific tool in many occasions such as the following examples:

- **Human and faunal fossils**: [a] restoring entire or part of an individual when the remains are scattered or missing: it allows fulfilling a material for study and comparison, and for conducting trials of incomplete fossils reconstruction. [b] replicating an entire specimen to be set in scientific expositions environments or to be transported to other institutions;
- **Portable art and bone industry**: [a] reconstitution of an artefact in order to prevent from being manually manipulated while being examined, thus preserving the original; [b] avoidance of transporting original fragile material between scientific institutions; [c] possibility that a researcher from afar can work the pieces; [d] recognition of tooling traceology in studies over shaped bone and lithic surfaces.
- **Archaeology in general**: [a] the molding of traces of human or animal activities (particularly in soils cave); footprints, handprints; ground drawings, animal paths, tool marks; entire settlement layers; [b] building a replica, sometimes in smaller scale, of structures; [c] replacing

an artefact to be partially or fully destroyed by dating processes: archaeological documents destined to destructive procedures are also conserved in the form of casting; [d] imprint of stratigraphic sections; [e] preservation of the image of the conditions of an object before restoration.

In many ways, a collection of moulages brings to life ancient artefacts in peerless ways. Photographs are useful, but they are two-dimensional, lacking the interactivity, and even the joyful activity of the three-dimensional object. Roughly, we distinguish four major areas in which the casting will play an essential role: heritage preservation, museology, education and research. Each of these areas requires great discipline throughout the work that will lead to the obtainment of a particular artefact facsimile.

3. A comparison between originals and replicas

3.1. Examination issues

Portable art objects have demonstrated to be sensitive to analyses regarding their physical aspects when applied on replicas. The identification of the anatomical and taxonomical criteria is a huge problem on casts, since it depends on the characteristics of morphology, texture, coloration and volume to be well recognized, and these features are far from flawless in bad quality moulages. Roughly 14% of the pieces from the collection is composed by raw material of unclear classification; a high number for this sort of work. Perhaps, if all the original pieces were available for study, the artefacts classified with imprecise tags could be successfully identified. As a matter of fact, the access to the documentation of the authentic pieces would solve the issue, but they are inexistent. Another point of the results that help us to tackle this issue is the condition of the facsimile objects; the majority presented fair quality (54%), only 28 (14%) of the moulages were considered in good conditions, and 65 replicated pieces – a worrisome 32% – were deemed as in poor condition. Our thoughts on these particular conditions over the replicas led to the comparative study over original and copied artefacts of the concerned collection. In this respect, all these circumstances challenged us to test if the collection was indeed reliable to be tackled in a laboratorial study.

Condition	No. Pieces	%
Mean	110	54%
Bad	65	32%
Good	28	14%
Total	203	100%

TABLE 1. NUMBER OF REPLICATED OBJECTS SORTED BY THEIR CONDITION.

In order to test the quality of the analyses made over the replicated pieces, nine authentic artefacts of portable art were chosen following the remarkableness of each piece for the goals of the work. We are going to see next that the characteristics of the supports are the most diagnosed issues when it comes to differentiate copies from genuine artefacts. Another point to stress out is the weight of the replicas; considering only scientific aspects, the difference in weight doesn't really have issues, but when it comes to pedagogical interests the weight is a important point on the handling of the artefact. Experimentation experts have already stressed that the choosing of determined raw materials rather than others might have close relations with the weight and the task for which that tool is aimed for (David, 2007).

3.2. Comparative analyses

Although nine artefacts were analyzed, for this paper, three examples were chosen to illustrate the comparisons between original artefacts and their respective copies: respectively, a uncouth, a satisfactory, and an superior replica.

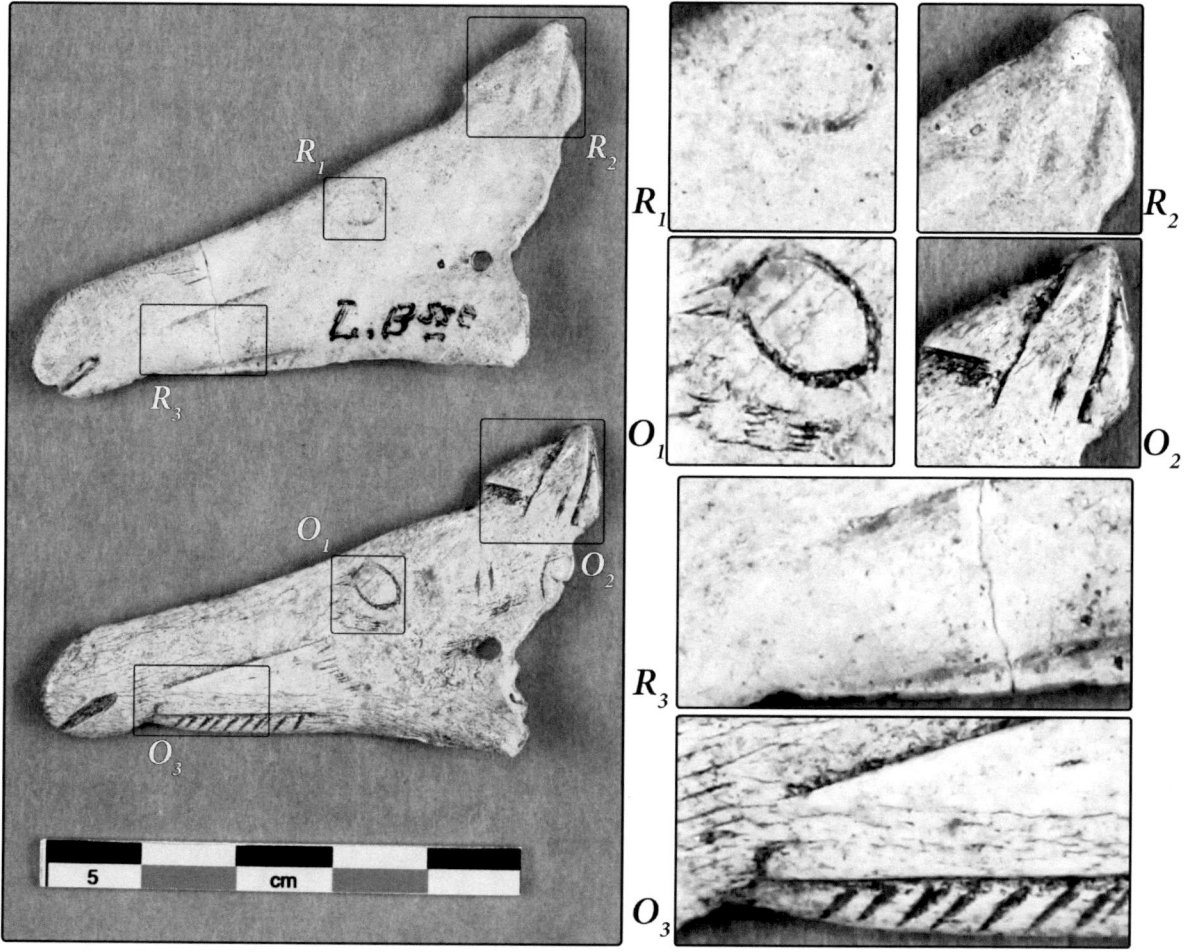

FIGURE 1. ARTEFACT USUALLY DENOMINATED "CONTOUR DECOUPÉ" MADE OF HYOID BONES. IT IS NORMALLY ASSOCIATED TO ADORNMENTS. LEFT PHOTO: PANORAMA DISPLAYING BOTH THE REPLICA (ABOVE) AND ORIGINAL (BELOW); RIGHT PHOTOS: DETAILS FROM THE SAME ZONES FEATURING THE DECORATIVE ASPECTS FROM BOTH OBJECTS. R = DETAILS FROM REPLICA; O = DETAILS FROM ORIGINAL. PHOTOS AND LAYOUT: R. AVILA.

Contour découpé (Figure 1)

"Contours découpés" are themselves very enigmatic artefacts for archaeologists. In contrast to "batons percés", that present numerous hypotheses of utilization, no features on them suggest numerous kinds of activities or functionalities they could have been used to. Most of them were made on hyoid bones, hardly achievable if lacking effort. Furthermore, the difficulty in their exploitation is often associated to a very selective procurement for a material that, as implied, wouldn't be used with a very relevant functional use. This means that if they were so important so that prehistoric men wasted so much time and energy to obtain it, but at the same time these artefacts have no practical functionality, so they must have had a very important symbolic significance. In our case, the artefact presents roughly 6.5 cm length and 0.5 width; it is truly frail. Therefore, working on its shaping and decoration is no easy task, and might have required not only thorough work, but mostly it might have requested a very talented craftsman.

Addressing the comparative analysis, the difference in weight between both objects is almost irrelevant, but it is noteworthy that the replica is heavier. Such object is a lean replication; the discrepancies of itself in relation to the genuine artefact are enormous. Firstly, the replica does not retain any property from the original support (grooves darker than the whitish surface of the piece), precluding any reliable anatomical and taxonomic recognition. The original piece displays smaller thickness and width, in spite of its longer length. About decorations, they are the greatest "disappointment" as the ones on the replica displays severe poverty in details. The original object is garnished by plenty of well marked traces on the ears (R_2 & O_2) and mouth of the represented animal, with heavy and precise incisions in the eye (R_1 & O_1), besides several parallel incisions on the nose and on the "goatee" (R_3 & O_3), perhaps intending to give the idea of bristles. Two curious details may demonstrate the negligence in the care over to the moulage: [1] the registration number – though hardly identifiable itself –that takes up a large part of one of the object's faces; [2] the replica features a fissure (figures R_3 & O_3) that doesn't exist on the original. These conditions maybe indicate a "lack of importance" given to the copied piece. Another relevant issue is that the drilling of the original object is quite larger than the one on the replica, which could be construed in different manners as to any scientific analysis. Different dimensions in perforations from different objects – or even in the same artefact – could suggest, erroneously, different functions for each of them. No characteristics of the replica could be used undoubtedly, so the copy is totally disposable if considered their scientific and educational values.

Baton percé 1 (Figure 2)

This artefact, found in the site of Laugerie Basse, in the Eyzies-de-Tayac, is remarkably carved in deer antler. Further references on it can be seen at the work of André Rigaud (Rigaud 2001). It can be set both as bone industry as portable art, mainly because the function(s) of "baton percés" are not yet settled: some associate them with symbolic functions (e.g. as symbols of high hierarchy and power) whilst others assign them to functional activities (e.g. auxiliary tool for throwing weapons). Regarding the comparison between original and copy, the first noteworthy issue has relation to their weights: the original artefact – made on antler – is lighter than the plaster replica, although both share almost exactly dimensions. It is also notable that some natural traits of the original piece, probably action of taphonomical agents, are overly marked on the moulage by the color tone (R_2 & O_2), which also features two massive traits that are, likely, a result of mold production. The characteristics of the support at the extremities are quite faithful (R_1 & O_1) but some details are lacking on the perforated zone – though nothing really worrisome. Yet, even if no compared to the original, physical features maintained on the moulage are so anchored that the recognition of the raw material is made with no problems. However, still in respect to the support, the most noticeable difference is the discrepancy in color between the pieces; whereas the original has grayish-white coloring, the copy is primarily brownish. Moreover, the lower contrasts of the replica difficult the identification of some decorations. In my perspective, this condition greatly compromises the didactic question of the replica. Roughly speaking, if a lay person observes the replica without being able to compare to the original, it will fatefully have the sensation that the original artefact features – if not the same coloration – at least a similar staining represented in the cast. Furthermore, the restoration made on the breakage of the authentic piece is not well replicated at the copy (R_3 & O_3). In spite of these latter conditions, both objects present quite similar textures, in addition to the flawless representation of decorations. Overall, the cast is fairly accurate to the authentic artefact, especially in its dimensions, decorations and for it keeps much of the characteristics of the support. The replica complies nicely with its role, both scientifically and pedagogically.

Mandible of cervid (Figure 3)

This piece was joined to the comparison for three reasons: 1 – The unusual anatomical part used in portable art (jaw); 2 – The peculiar and rare decoration of a fish in full body with the intent to represent it in a realistic fashion; 3 – The extraordinarily quality of reproduction of the original artefact. Here again, the original piece is the lightest. Many features of the support are quite well represented, although the regions of the teeth are not absolutely loyal and there are lacks of minimal

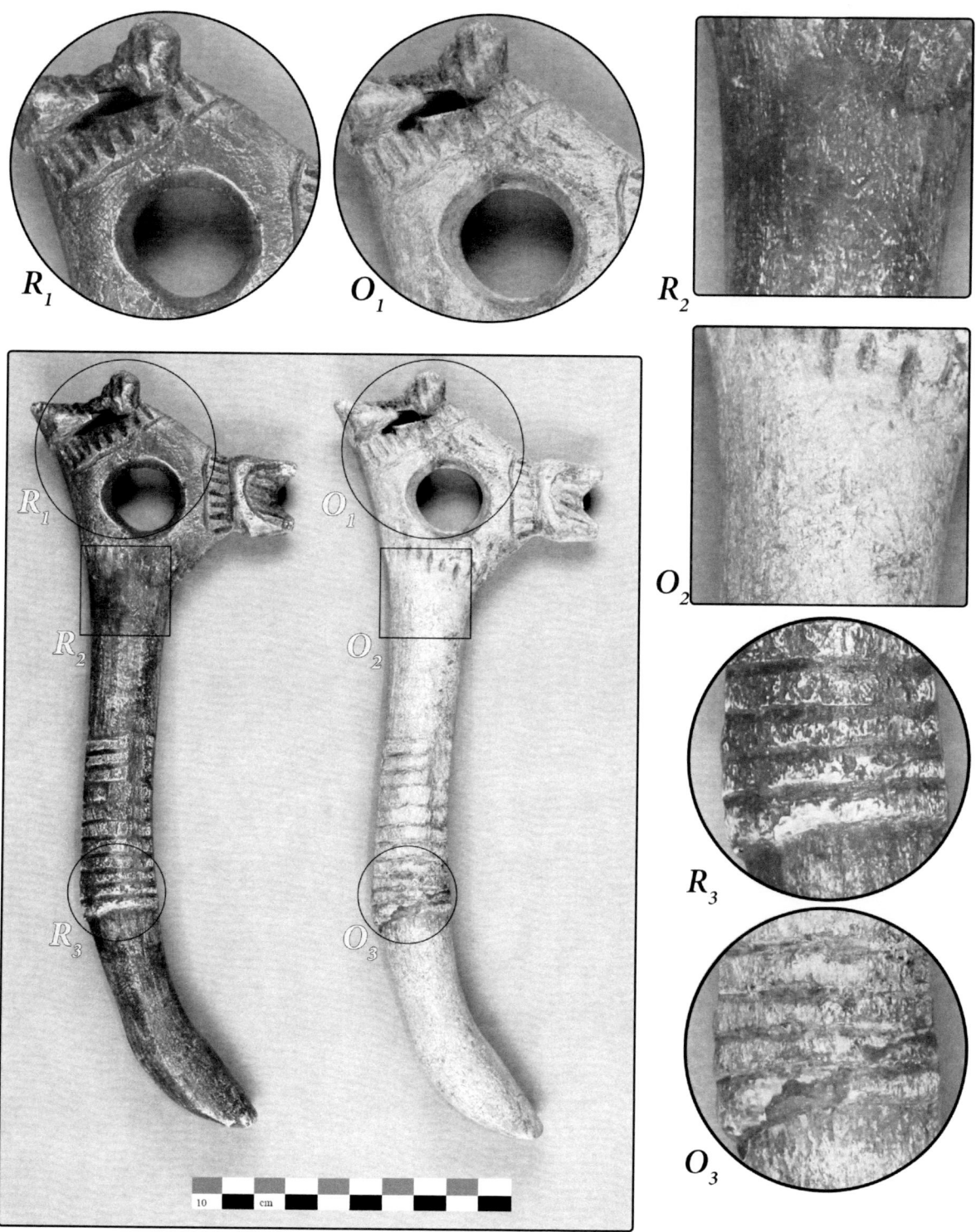

FIGURE 2. ARTEFACT USUALLY DENOMINATED "BÂTON PERCÉ", MADE ON ANTLER. LARGEST PICTURE: PANORAMA DISPLAYING BOTH THE REPLICA (LEFT) AND ORIGINAL (RIGHT); SMALLER PHOTOS: DETAILS FROM THE SAME ZONES OF BOTH OBJECTS FEATURING THEIR DIFFERENCES AND SIMILARITIES. R = DETAILS FROM REPLICA; O = DETAILS FROM ORIGINAL. PHOTOS AND LAYOUT: R. AVILA.

details, such as cracks, in the bone surface (R_1 & O_1). The more yellowish tinge of the replica is another downer, but the natural toning of the original object is not missing; in other words, there were

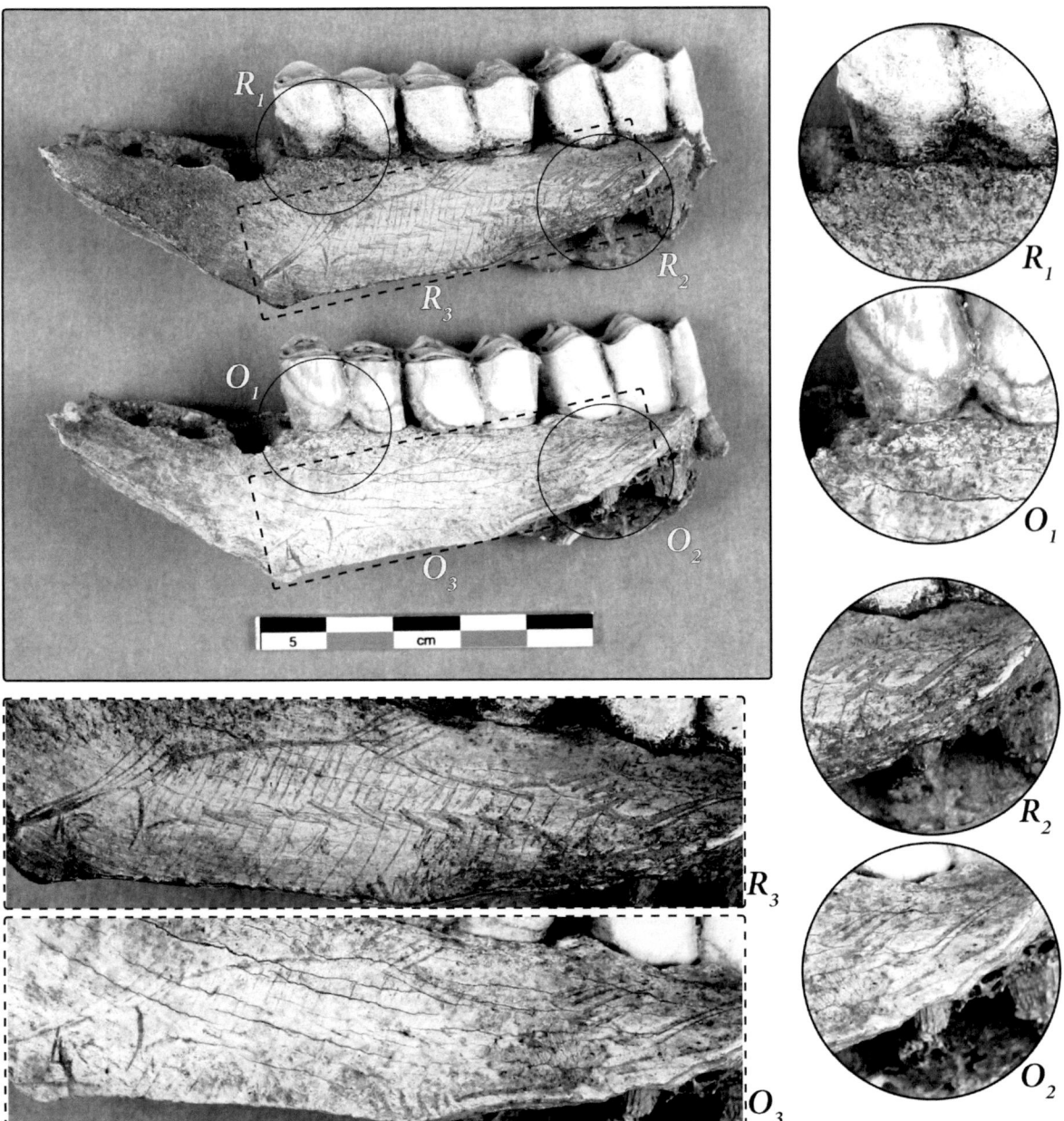

FIGURE 3. ARTEFACT WITH NO APPARENT FUNCTION MADE ON A MANDIBLE OF CERVID. LARGEST: PANORAMA DISPLAYING BOTH THE REPLICA (ABOVE) AND ORIGINAL (BELOW); SMALLER: DETAILS FROM THE SAME ZONES OF BOTH OBJECTS FEATURING THEIR DIFFERENCES AND LIKENESSES. R = DETAILS FROM REPLICA; O = DETAILS FROM ORIGINAL. PHOTOS AND LAYOUT: R. AVILA.

efforts in reproducing every detail, but the difference in coloration is always present. Furthermore, the moulage is faithful enough to allow the observation of taphonomic alterations of the original piece (sediment encrusted on its surface) and the broken edges of the piece are virtually identical to the original (R_2 & O_2). Regarding the decoration of the fish, due to the high contrast, the incisions are much clearer in the replica than the original (R_3 & O_3). Given the difficulty in representing such a particular piece, it can be considered an excellent replica for didactic purposes, though also responds greatly to its scientific nature.

3.3. Conclusions over the comparison

The addressed replicas proved to be proper to their current applications: teaching, divulgation and research. The majority could be used in any of these activities, but they are more restricted in relation to the scientific environment. The reason is that scientific studies are based in objectivity and exhaustiveness of their analyses, but the latter cannot be fully provided by replicas – unless they and their respective original artefacts are exceptionally well documented; a rather rare condition. As we saw in the examination problems, replicas of portable art have demonstrated to be sensitive when analyses of their physical aspects were tackled. In the comparative study we confirmed this difficulty, since some of the replicas didn't provide enough characteristics to reliably recognize different kinds of materials, neither to identify anatomical parts and taxonomies. These circumstances make us ponder in which degree replicas could be used in analyses when their physical features are critical to the results of the work – essentially, researches concerning anatomical and taxonomical recognition.

Although recognition of natural physical aspects can be imprecise, when the concern comes to be direct human activity on the pieces – techno-typology and decoration – replicas do not show major problems in providing enough information. Regarding portable art, this could mean three things: [1] that human activity is more diagnostic than natural conditions; [2] that molders concentrate more in aspects related to human factors; maybe because they can understand it better; [3] or that the fabrication of replicas is a poor technique if related to natural characteristics. In fact, the last one may not be the most likely, once casts for longer have proved to be a powerful tool in natural sciences for reproducing fossils, bones, and so forth. Howsoever, replicas have shown to carry the same load of information as the original artefacts do, and in a surprisingly reliable manner; therefore moulages may be used as fruitful as the originals, whether at studies addressing typology or iconography.

4. Final considerations

This study had two main focuses that, in the end, came to be complementary: the descriptive analysis of prehistoric portable art pieces and scientific concerns on their replicated artefacts. This dialogical relationship proved to be deeper than it priory seemed, bringing on plenty of other problematic over documentation, contextualization, conservation, and museology, among other epistemological questions in archaeology. Furthermore, concerns over the role of replicas into such analysis and their scientific and educational values have emerged. Thus, a comparison between a sample of the replicas previously addressed and their respective original artefacts was offered. The results showed that studies based upon replicas are perfectly reasonable as to decorative and symbolic features, but display problems regarding the physical and structural aspects of the pieces.

However, if moulages demonstrate not being completely reliable, shouldn't scholars avoid replicas? How can we work on these issues when the originals are not available? The answer is rather simple: through the documentation of the original. Actually, it is a question of documentation and contextualization: both must provide clear information on the relation between moulages and original artefacts. In other words, casts must have in their own record a space for their own contextualization and equivalent data related to their respective original. This uncomplicated – but arduous – task of compiling data from dispersed documents would avoid mistakes regarding subjectivity over physical aspects, and would also save the hassle of future researchers who wouldn't need to bother profoundly with material analysis. Once that all data linking replica and original is successfully aggregated, any imprecision and dubiousness about the replica is sorted out, thus providing all the resources the piece itself cannot offer.

A well documented piece is always fundamental for any museological study, but it comes to be unavoidable in regard to collections of portable art casts. In these cases, an ideal documentation should contain subjects of contextualization extrinsic to the artefact such as management numbers, authors, dates of conditioning and restoring, and so forth; and issues intrinsic to the artefact, in other

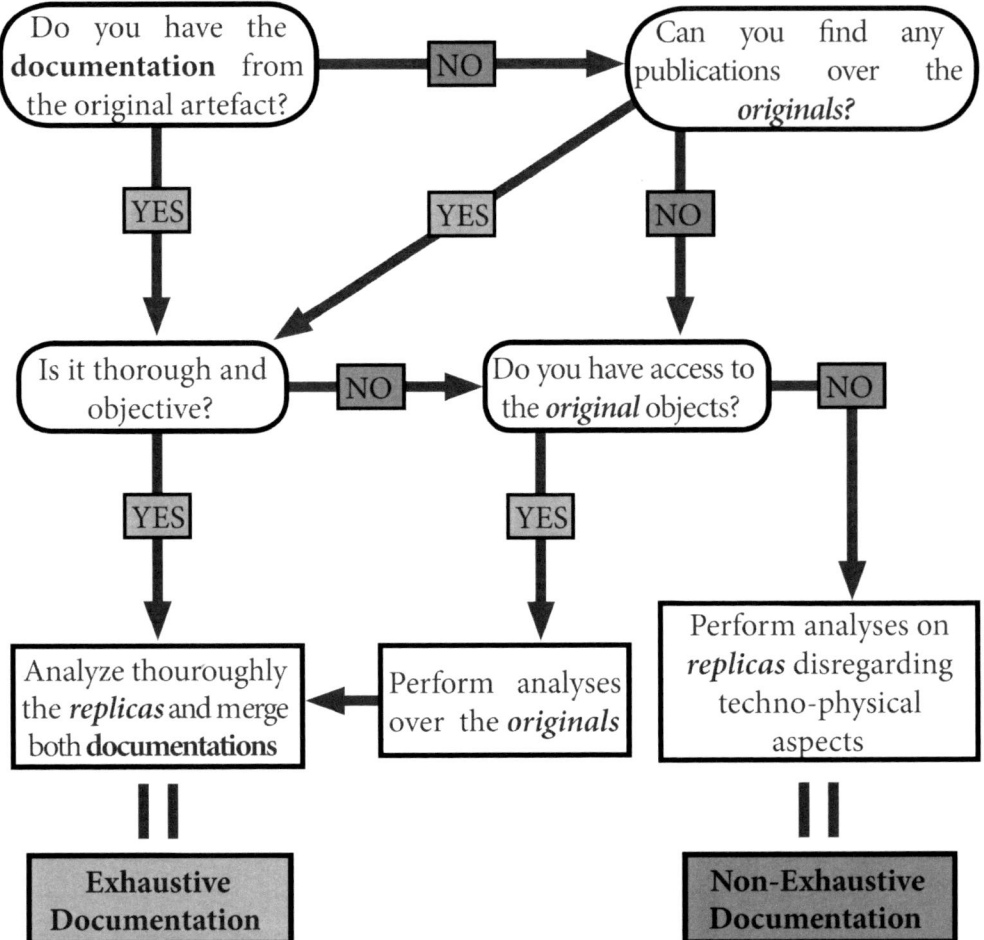

FIGURE 4. FLOWCHART OF AN EXHAUSTIVE DOCUMENTATION RELATED TO PORTABLE ART REPLICAS.

words, the information that one could extract from the observation and analysis of the object itself, i.e., natural aspects of the material and its consequent identifications (support, anatomy, taxonomy, taphonomy, etc), anthropic actions (data related to typology and decoration), along with others. The idea of such documentation must be to contextualize and link replicas to their respective original artefacts in order to learn things that are not readable or workable uniquely with the copy. Such as any other archaeological object, copies cannot tell us much if we do not have a good context. The issue is quite clear: if archaeological objects need contextualization, so do replicas; if they are legitimate reproductions of those archaeological objects, so they need exactly the same contextual information; finally, in the same way that we have notions on the "chaîne opératoire" of such archaeological objects, we would have the same kind of data over moulages.

Thereby, departing from the original, its analyses will provide information to the creation of documentation. The manufacturing of the replica from the original also offers its own documentation (historical, scientific, and so forth). Then, if replicas are to be studied, they will have to dialogue with both records in order to create a proper and suitable data. And so, assuming that the findings of the study on the replica are good, the information generated by it can be added to the previous documentation; in return, the comparison between the two outcomes (original x replica) might even develop new hypotheses and challenge old paradigms.

References

ANTONINI, L. 2012. La fragilité immatérielle comme paramètre de la conservation préventive: l'exemple de la collection de moulages du musée des Monuments français. In Situ [En ligne], 19, 2012, mis en ligne le 01 octobre 2012, consulté le 15 juin 2014. URL: http://insitu.revues.org/9900; DOI:10.4000/insitu.9900

ÁVILA, R. 2014. Magdalenian portable art: analysis of a collection from Dordogne and reflections over its replicas. 87 p. Master disseration. Paris: Department of Prehistory, Muséum National d'Histoire Naturelle.

BARBANERA, M. 2000. Les collections de moulages au XIXe siècle: étapes d'un parcours entre idéalisme, positivisme et esthétisme. In Henri, L.; François, Q., éds.- Les Moulages de sculptures antiques et l'histoire de l'archéologie. Actes du colloque international Paris, (24 octobre 1997). EPHE, IVe section Sciences historique et philologique III Hautes études du Monde gréco-romain 29. Genève: DROZ, p. 57-73.

CROCQUEVIEILLE, G. 2008. Les moulages d'après l'antique de la Cour Vitrée de l'École des Beaux-arts de Paris. Histoire de leur présentation dans la cours centrale du Palais des Études (1876-1970) et leur identification au sein des collections des Écuries du Roy à Versailles. 60 p. Mémoire d'étude. Volume 1: texte, École du Louvre.

DAVID, É. 2007. Technology on Bone and Antler industries: A Relevant Methodology for Characterizing Early Post-Glacial Societies (9th-8th Millennium BC). In St.-Pierre, Ch. G.; Walker, R., eds.- Bones as Tools; Current methods and interpretations in worked bone studies. Oxford: Archaeopress, p. 35-50. (B.A.R. International Series; 1622).

FALSER, M. 2011. Krishna and the Plaster Cast. Translating the Cambodian Temple of Angkor Wat in the French Colonial Period. Transcultural Studies, Heidelberg [Online]. Número 2, p. 6-50 [Last access in 03/07/2014]. Available at URL: http://journals.ub.uni-heidelberg.de/index.php/transcultural/article/view/9083

RIGAUD, A. 2001. Les bâtons percés: décors énigmatiques et fonction possible. Gallia Préhistoire. Tome 43, p. 101-151.